Look at Them This way

Look at Them This Way

Some Old Testament stories revisited

Norman Price

EPWORTH PRESS

British Library Cataloguing in Publication Data

Price, Norman, *1926–*
Look at them this way: some Old Testament stories
revisited.
1. Bible. O. T. – Critical studies
I. Title
221.6

ISBN 0–7162–0464–9

First published 1989
by Epworth Press, Room 195, 1 Central Buildings
Westminster, London SW1H 9NR

Phototypeset by J&L Composition Ltd, Filey
and printed in Great Britain by
Richard Clay Ltd, Bungay, Suffolk

Contents

Introduction

'What is truth'? asked Pontius Pilate, when he was questioning Jesus (John 18.38), but did not wait for an answer. What that answer might have been we can only surmise, but certainly that same question has been asked many times since, often in connection with the contents of the Bible and in particular some of the stories found in the Old Testament. 'Is this *really* true'? is the frequent re-action to the reading of them, with the implication that the questioner will not be prepared to take 'Yes' for an answer. Possibly, like Pilate, questioners will not wait for an answer, but if they are sincere in their quest the reply must carefully qualify exactly what is meant by 'truth', otherwise the consequence may be a refusal to ever take the Bible seriously again. Many a person has grown up with the most disastrous and derisory ideas of what the book is about because someone, somewhere along the line, gave them the wrong answers to the right questions.

Whenever I am asked about the actual truth of certain Old Testament stories, which in my teaching career was very frequently, I reply, 'Of course they are true, providing you are quite clear as to what kind of truth you are looking for.' Truths have always been conveyed in many forms and facets, and as far as some of these Old Testament stories and characters are concerned, we must first separate such things as symbolism, parable, poetry, hyperbole, myth and folk-story, from that which is not. These are the tools of the trade of all great creative writers, of every race and generation, and the Bible writers, who include some of the greatest the world has ever seen, are no exception. We must allow them the freedom to use these many mediums to portray their particular truths and must not persist in taking literally that which was never intended to be taken as such and then, having accepted that, we can move on to examine the vital moral, social and religious truths which the stories contain and which are just as valid as any other kind.

When we recognize this, the Bible writers, through their superb craftsmanship and skill, will provide paths that will lead to the very mountain tops and which will show us the kind of view we can never enjoy from the foothills of extreme fundamentalism.

People sometimes point to archaeology as support for 'proving', or even 'disproving' the Bible record, and certainly a great deal of extremely valuable work has been done in this respect, especially in this present century, but it would be rash to claim too much credit for such discoveries. Biblical archaeology has thrown a lot of light on the general context of the ancient world and has made it less difficult to accept some scriptural stories than may have been the case previously, but having said that, we must remember that there are many parts of the Bible which are quite outside the scope of the spade to discover. The Bible does not stand or fall simply by the degree of historical accuracy in the events it deals with. The writers were not primarily concerned with improving our science, or history or geography. They were dealing with other dimensions of life and we must never try to tether these superb craftsmen to the merely mundane. The claim of the Bible to be the word of God does not rest on establishing the historicity of its contents, but rather on the realization of the reality of the experience of God which is offered in it. Otherwise, it is like trying to judge the work of a great artist merely by the pigments in the paint.

It is sometimes said that young people have the ability to

'walk round' within a story and then discover for themselves 'layers of meaning' as they mature. This is no doubt true of some, but one meets many people who, as far as the Bible is concerned at least, have 'walked into' certain parts of it when they were young, but far from discovering much meaning, have instead become enmeshed in a maze which has left them bothered and bewildered ever since, with the very real possibility that they may develop an attitude which will never treat the Bible with much respect or interest again.

With all this in mind, I have selected some familiar Old Testament stories, often derided and dismissed as fanciful and far-fetched, and invite readers to take a new look at them as far as certain aspects of truth are concerned. One is not trying to revive controversies or to re-enact new theories, but simply attempting to restore some very valuable 'antiques' to what, in my view at least, seems to be their 'originals'. In which case, perhaps this little book may be a means of 'walking into' the stories, instead of walking away from them.

1

Adam and Eve

The most honest way into a house, besides being often the most interesting, is usually by way of the front door. By the same token, one could say that the best place to begin in taking a fresh look at some of the rather 'odd' Old Testament Stories, is at the beginning, with the stories of Creation. Not that they were written at the beginning, but because they are about the beginnings they were put at the beginning, as the opening chapters of Genesis. The word 'Genesis' means 'beginning' and some manuscripts give it its full title of 'Genesis Kosmou', which means 'Origins of the World'. One manuscript calls it 'The Book of Origins', whilst in the Hebrew Bible it is simply headed 'Bereshith', which means 'In the Beginning'.

Whichever title one may prefer, the book tells us of the origins of many things, at least as far as the writers saw them. One uses the word 'writers' because although for many centuries it was accepted that Moses was almost certainly the sole author not only of Genesis, but of all the first five books in the Bible, known as the Pentateuch, (from the Greek 'teuchos' = scroll and 'penta' = five), it is now generally accepted that there were several authors involved. The 'break-through' came in 1655, when a French scholar, Isaac de la Peyrére, published a pamphlet presenting the thesis that the

1

Pentateuch was, in fact, the work of more than one writer. Peyrére was arrested by the Inquisition and his book publically burned, but his ideas had taken root and what became known as the 'Documentary Theory' is widely taught. Briefly, and in simply literary terms, this states that the Pentateuch took shape in a series of stages in which, over several centuries, four distinct documents, written at different times by different writers, were brought together by various editors, or 'redactors', to form a single work. These sources have come to be denoted by the letters, J, E, P and D, with J and E being so called because of the way they prefer the use of the divine names Jahweh and Elohim, P being marked by the style and interests of the priestly circle and D consisting mainly of material found in the book of Deuteronomy.

Having said that, it must be pointed out that modifications and criticisms of this theory are continually being made. For example, a recent study by the Israel Institute of Technology in Haifa, which entailed the feeding of some 20,000 words of Genesis into computers and thereby conducting an analysis of its language make-up, claimed that 'The probability of Genesis having but one author is statistically high', but then went on to say that 'Whilst the J and E narratives seemed to be linguistically indistinguishable, the P sections differed widely from them.' Also, some scholars suspect that far from the sources J, E, and D being the work of single authors, their origins and construction are extremely complicated. Some even doubt whether they were ever 'documents' at all, or whether they were 'streams of oral tradition', whilst Professor R. N. Whybray, in his recent book, 'The Making of the Pentateuch', argues that the Pentateuch is the work of a single sixth-century historian, who compiled a history of his nation's origins by drawing upon his own literary imagination or upon folklore current in his own time.

However, the Documentary Hypothesis has enjoyed widespread recognition for over a hundred years, ever since the German theologian Julius Wellhausen first put forward his classic exposition in 1876 and so for the purpose of this chapter, which does not profess to be an examination of the sources of the Pentateuch, we can continue to identify the writers by their initial letters. We can also, I think, work on the largely accepted premise that the writers were looking back on the origins of the Hebrew faith and religion from the viewpoint of many years later than Moses. In other words, they were re-writing the early stories in the light of what was happening to their nation at the time of writing.

In a broadcast programme on the various theories of Creation, entitled *Genesis Fights Back*, one speaker began with the question, 'Are you aware that there are, in fact, two accounts of Creation in the book of Genesis'? He wasn't being facetious ... he knew that there are many people who have never realized that fact. They have always assumed that the Bible says that God made all things in six days and Adam and Eve were the climax of that single story. Possibly they had been so busy dismissing the whole thing as bunkum that they had not noticed that there are two quite different accounts, evidently written by people from different backgrounds and with different aims and purposes in writng. Even a cursory comparison will show that the two versions are not the same in their order of creation. The first story has human beings appearing last, after all the plants and animals, whilst the second has them coming first.

The first story (1.1 – 2.3), is usually referred to as the 'P' account and in this context we should probably think of a school of priests who had been taken to Babylon from Jerusalem in the Exile of 586 BC. The other exiles had become so attracted to the beauty and splendours of Babylon ... the famous 'Hanging', or terraced Gardens, for example, were one of the Wonders of the Ancient World ... that some of them, at least, were tempted to join in the worship of the Babylonian gods. After all, ran the reasoning, the Babylonians seemed to be prospering a lot better than the Jews, so worship of their gods appeared a better proposition than the worship of Jehovah had been in Jerusalem, seeing that the city had been reduced to a sacked and smoking ruin.

To counteract such temptations and suppositions, and to strengthen the hope that the exiles would one day return to Jerusalem and to the true worship of God there, the writer reminds them of the great traditions of the past and the power and grandeur of the God who is the source and being of all things ... a God who is far greater than all the Babylonian gods put together. So he looks back to the very beginning of it all, to the Creation itself, and pens a superb poem on the creative power and purpose of the God who brought order out of chaos and light out of darkness by direction of his Spirit, then finally created humans to be responsible for the rest of creation. The poem culminates with another 'origin' ... that of the Sabbath, when God, having completed creation in six days, rested on the seventh day, so the Hebrew word for 'rest' – 'Shabath' – was given to that day. The fact that P connects the origin of the Sabbath not just with the history of Israel, but with Creation itself, represents its observance as a fundamental law of the world order, even though, in fact, the question of the actual origins of the festival amongst the early, nomadic Israelites is very complicated and obscure. The writer seems to re-interpret a custom which had its origins in a much more primitive view of things. The realization of this kind of 'reading back' by later writers is, in my view, the vital key to this particular box of truths.

Of the two accounts of Creation, the first is often regarded as 'fairly factual' by those people who say they don't want to be too scientific or too sceptical, and the second as fables and fairy tales by those who say they do want to be scientific and, so they maintain, sensible too. One often reads and hears of these stories being described, or dismissed, as 'myths and legends', and many think this gives them the right to regard them as absolute fiction and product of someone's fertile but fatuous imagination. This is the first step in the wrong direction, because to describe something as a 'myth' does not mean that it is wholly untrue or merely imaginative, despite the dictionary definition of 'myth' as 'a purely fictitious narrative, usually involving supernatural persons or events'.

The Creation stories in Genesis can be called 'myths' because they are the kind of story whose truths are quite outside the scope of history and whose mystery is the 'myth story', as it were. Profound moral, social and theological truths have always been expressed in this form, by people of all races and languages, and these Bible stories are no exception. They may not be historical in the kind of concrete context in which we usually use that word, but the truths and lessons they try to teach are forever valid for the very reason that they cannot be bound by an historical situation. A story does not have to be historical for the lesson to be true. If it were, a lot of the world's greatest literature would have to be labelled 'untrue' and the writers regarded as deceivers rather than divulgers of deepest thoughts and ideas.

As far as the first Creation story goes, a great deal of hot air, not to say holy smoke, has been generated since Darwin's famous theory of evolution published in 1859. There was a story of the bishop's wife who, on hearing this idea of humanity's origins, exclaimed, 'Descended from apes! One trusts that it is not true, but if it is, that it will not become widely known.' But it did become 'widely known' and what is sometimes called the 'Monkey War' has been raging, on and off, ever since. Darwin's own prediction, that his ideas may 'prove distasteful to some' became the understatement of the age. In certain parts of America those who dared teach such notions were hanged in effigy and to the already listed 'sins' of 'drinking, dancing and gambling' were added the further 'sin' of belief in evolution! Moreover, there are signs that the war between the creationists and evolutionists is being waged today as strongly as ever. A recent Gallop Poll conducted in America showed that of all the adults questioned, about half said that they believed 'God started the human race with the creation of Adam and Eve', and there is increasing pressure in their schools for biology books to give equal emphasis to the teaching of both points of view. Not so in Britain. Not so long ago, a teacher of Religious Education was actually dismissed from his post by a certain Education Authority for 'contravening the agreed syllabus' by teaching that God created the world in six days. Perhaps he was an ardent fundamentalist, but one rather wonders whether if he had been using his RE lessons to belittle every biblical belief in sight, far from being punished, he may well have been applauded, or possibly promoted!

The full title of Darwin's ideas and observations was *The Origin of Species by means of Natural Selection, or The Preservation of Favoured Races in the Struggle for Life*, and some would maintain that there is a grave danger of some extreme racial and political groups pouncing on these ideas to 'prove' their particular propaganda and points of view. It is not difficult to see how the 'favoured races' philosophy could lead to support of slavery, apartheid, oppression and discrimination of many kinds, and there are those who maintain that Hitler used the idea to qualify his desire for a 'master' race, with the concentration camps and gas chambers becoming the 'final solution' to the problem of 'natural selection'. Others interpret the ideas as meaning the survival of the fittest, with its attendant policies of letting the weakest go to the wall. Certainly, the concept of evolution does not necessarily carry with it many lofty ideas of morality and human history does not appear to vindicate the beliefs of some evolutionists that as human beings 'evolve', they automatically make moral as well as material progress. To some people, the step between thinking of humans as little more than animals, and then treating them as such, is a very short one.

However, to engage in heated arguments about the creation poem of P, who, as far as I can discover, never made the slightest claim to being a scientist, then to say that science and religion are at loggerheads over the issues, is a pointless pastime and is certainly barking up the wrong tree. We shall miss the whole point of the poems and parables if we persist in regarding them either as literal truth or as primitive guesses at scientific fact. How can there be conflict between science and the opening chapters of Genesis when the two are talking about different things? This assumption of opposition and contradiction has been largely brought about by people who persist in misunderstanding the nature of the Genesis stories. In any case, science is not infallible, and there were scientists who after seeing the pictures sent back by satellites from outer space, said 'We shall have to re-write the text-books.' To imagine that a truth is only 'true' when it can be 'proved' by scientific methods is to imply that, for example, a religious and moral truth can only be mere opinion.

In 1660, Archbishop James Ussher of Armagh in Ireland, basing his calculations on all the figures given in the bible for the age of Adam and his descendants, arrived at the conclusion that the earth was created in 4004 BC, on the 22 October and at 6 o'clock in the evening! If we reject that calculation ... and all but the most fanatical fundamentalists appear to do so ... what are we left with? Did humanity evolve painfully and slowly over countless millions of years, from some kind of proto-primate, tree-dwelling mammal, to 'Homo-erectus', then to 'Homo-sapiens', and then gradually spreading all over the world, or was it a separate part of Creation? Were there long periods of stability, then 'sudden jumps', or bursts of creative activity, which then produced new species in particular places ... a kind of 'localized' Darwinism ... or was evolution a much faster process than most evolutionists imagine, or even perhaps on a much smaller scale? Some scientists are more specific. The late Professor Jacob Bronowski, in his television Series, *The Ascent of Man*, said he could pinpoint the actual birthplace of the human race as being the river valley of the Omo in Ethiopia.

To all these ideas and theories Christians must pay close attention, and many may find no difficulty in believing that God's way of working may well have been very slow and gradual, although they see in all these explanations great areas of unsolved mysteries and inconsistencies, not least the enormous gap in terms of speech, consciousness and intelligence between humans and other living animals. This is not made any less difficult by so many investigations dealing with laws according to which nature *now* works, and not with the origin of those laws. The important thing is that if we leave God out of the reckoning, it is very difficult to give much guidance on origins at all.

Which is where P's stupendous poem comes in. It *is* concerned with origins and begins with one majestic, basic assumption: 'In the beginning God created the heaven and the earth.' He does not say when the 'beginning' was, because he does not know and is not concerned. He does not speak of 'Big Bangs', or billions of years. He is far more concerned with the question that people of all races and religions have always asked: 'How did this world and everything in it come into existence'?, and to that profound question he gives a simple, straightforward answer. It is all here because God made it all. The vital thing to the writer was not how we were created, but who created us and his answer may sound naive, but it is certainly not negative. It is, he says, God's world and God's handiwork. He not only puts God into the picture, he portrays him as the supreme painter, the creative artist, the mind and purpose behind the whole plan. P never contemplated any alternative. No doubt he would have thought that to maintain that there was no creator and no plan, and that the whole thing was some kind of haphazard astronomical accident *would* have sounded naive. After all, as one scientist put it, it takes a bit more than a wind blowing through a scrapyard to produce a jumbo jet!

Of course, one can find flaws in P's account, if we persist in looking at it merely from a scientific point of view. Although the writer seems to have got the order and sequence of creation about right – from darkness and water everywhere to the emergence of land and appearance of animals and humans – he believed that the earth was flat, the sky solid, and the sun, moon and stars mere lights up in the firmament. Also, despite the attempts to make the word mean something else, by 'day' he meant exactly what we mean. He wanted to give the ultimate example of God's greatness and power, and the significance of this was his ability to do so much in a single day.

So we may be tempted to scoff at the writer's science, but if we do so we must take care not to miss the 'punch-line' of the poem. If one goes to a symphony concert and concentrates only on the decibels or vibrations per second, it may give some kind of satisfaction, but it may also mean that one misses out on the Beethoven, which would be a tragedy. To try and find the secret of the song of a bird by dissecting the songster would be extremely foolish, since such an approach would only ensure that the secret had been lost altogether. So to sneer at the writer's science may give some satisfaction, but it may well mean that in doing so we fail to find his philosophy. The presentation is pictorial and parabolic, but the colours are clear and the poetry is perfect. Once, he says, there was deep darkness, disorder and chaos over the face of the earth, but then the creative spirit of God moved across the waters which covered the earth and out of the primaeval desolation he brought light and life and meaning. God saw that it was all good and one good thing led to another until the whole creation was crowned and culminated with the appearance of human beings.

So, according to the story, and to one translation, God created human beings, male and female, and 'making them like himself', or 'in his own image'. This was not a 'small edition' of God himself, as some sects claim, nor a 'little god', as some people seem to think of themselves, but being created in God's nature. Humanity was not only a work of art, but also a representation of God's divine rule and purpose on the earth. Human beings were to be 'like God' because they were to have the power of thought, communication and creativity, as well as having a special relationship with God the creator. The creation of humankind was invested with a special solemnity, for the story states that God first consulted with divine beings other than himself: 'Let us make man'. For this special act of creation, it was fitting that God should take counsel with the heavenly host and inaugurate co-operation from the whole company of heaven. It was a very high belief with a humble origin, but the opposite to that is the assumption that God is made in humanity's own image, which opens the way into a barren wilderness rather than a road to a more fruitful way of life and hope. The 'image' was seen as a heritage from God, but, as events were to show, it could be blurred and broken but restored by the process of redemption.

But then, the writer goes on to remind us, humanity was

9

not only given a special status, but also a special task, to be the trustee of God's good earth. Humans were not only the masterpiece of God's creation, they had special responsibility towards the rest of creation. They are caretakers of God's world, not exploiters and spoilers of it. Their job is to look after it on God's behalf. They have, as the writer puts it, 'dominion' over the rest of creation, but it is a power that must be tempered with a realization of responsibility. After God had created male and female, the story says that he 'blessed them and said to them ...' (v.28). Between God and humans there could be conversation and communication. Their place and position in creation was unique, and part of that special relationship was to be singled out as God's stewards. All this was not trite ... it was one of the great truths which the writer was trying to portray.

When we look at the second account of creation, in chapters two and three, we must surely ask ourselves whether the writer ever intended anyone to take his story literally. The 'science' is certainly very suspect, besides being 'backwards' compared to chapter one. This time, the earth is barren and bone-dry, the man is created before all the animals, and the woman is made from a piece of rib taken from the man whilst he is asleep. Then there is talk of 'a tree of life' and 'a tree of the knowledge of good and evil', and the whole thing begins to sound like a story about human nature, superb but very symbolic. Not an account of creation, nor an explanation of the origin of species, but an examination of the origins of evil, and this, in my view, is exactly what it was intended to be.

The writer, known by the letter J, was probably looking back from the time of King Solomon, c.950 BC, when that king, in an effort to improve his nation's economic position, had allowed all kinds of heathen ideas and practices to flourish in Jerusalem. It was a time of tolerance of policies that no doubt propagated a popular political image and many imagined that they had never had life so good, but in fact it was all achieved at tremendous cost, as far as the lives and liberty of many Israelites was concerned. Such was Solomon's 'wisdom'. The nation may have moved into a period of profitability as far as commerce was concerned, but it was plunged into moral bankruptcy as far as people were concerned, and the writer felt it was time to give some much-needed reminders on how people can become estranged from God through rebellion and desertion of God's demands. The rise of the monarchy had brought many radical changes and Israel found itself facing a religious crisis, and in that situation the J, or Yahwist writer, as some prefer to term it, accomplished a tremendous feat of literary and theological creativity. At the very time when the traditions of Moses were being threatened by the collapse of the old tribal, or Confederacy, system in Israel and the rise of syncretism under Solomon, he gave new expression to the faith of his fathers, and he began his epic with a 'Creation' account that shows, in vivid and symbolic style, how goodness and godliness can so easily degenerate through disobedience and deception. He wanted to show how quickly people can fall from grace and how God's purposes can be spoiled, and is therefore much more concerned with how people behave towards one another and towards God than in wondering how we got here in the first place.

So the writer begins to paint a wonderful parable picture, set in the scene of a garden. If he were a person used to the harshness of the wilderness, as he may well have been, then a lush, fertile, colourful 'paradise' was the most desirable place he could envisage. Many attempts have been made to locate this 'Eden' and to identify the four rivers mentioned, but all this is largely academic because the writer's spotlight is on people rather than on 'paradise'. The name 'Adam' may have come from the Assyrian word 'adamu', meaning 'to make', but more likely it is a play on the Hebrew word 'adamah', which meant 'ground'. So 'Adam' was the man of the earth and soil. He represented Everyman, not an individual. He was 'man' in general not in particular, and was told that he had the freedom of the garden to eat any of the fruit, except that from the tree 'of the knowledge of good and evil'. If he ate from that, he was told, he would die. It was a fair warning and the man seemed to heed it.

11

Then, in the story, came the complications and, in my view, some very deep insights into human experience from the writer. God decided that 'It is not good for the man to be alone.' He was made for friendship and fellowship, not isolation. So a 'companion' and partner had to be found, with whom the man could have 'responsible relations', which is what the word 'helpmeet' actually means. Furthermore, when the 'woman' was created, she was taken from Adam's rib and side, which, in my view, is significant and symbolic to the extent that she was seen as being by his side, a fitting help, a sharer in his life and experience. Obviously, one must bear in mind that J wrote in a man-dominated world, where women were, and often still are, regarded as weaker, though not necessarily inferior, to men and he has no compunction in implying that it was through this companion that temptation gained admittance to the garden party, but he also maintains that there was no completion apart from her creation.

It was Adam's sensitivity, not his sense of superiority that let the woman influence him. She was to be known as 'Eve', from the word 'Havvah', meaning 'Living', or 'Giver of life', and here the writer faces up to the age-old question of human sexual relationships. If the race is to survive, and people are to propagate, then there must obviously be sexual attraction and activity. But such a relationship must be safe-guarded and sanctified, and related religiously to life. It is a power and force that can and does arouse the fiercest passions and foulest crimes, but which can also express the deepest and most endearing of human relationships. Therein lies its problems, and its possibilities and perversions.

They are problems which, as far as one can understand, are peculiar to the human race, because it is the coming together of two different personalities to give and to receive the utmost that they share with each other. Such relationships must have a mutuality and discipline, or else they will never reach their full potential or purpose. Those who want to undermine an otherwise law-abiding and stable society know only too well that the first step towards it is the breaking down of mutual dignity and self-respect, individually and collectively, thereby creating an attitude and atmosphere in which people can be regarded as exploitable and expendable. The easiest and quickest way to achieve this aim is the encouragement and condoning of casual and irresponsible attitudes towards sexual relationships. Such a dangerous diet has resulted in many a sick society throughout human history. The prophets of the Old Testament saw the fate which befell Samaria and Jerusalem as being brought about much more by the worship of Astarte and Baal, with all its emphasis on the erotic, than by the efforts of the Assyrians and Babylonians, and there is little doubt that the decline and fall of the Roman Empire was due far more to immoralities and perversions of every kind than to the action of enemy armies. A great tree blown down by the wind is often seen as having internal decay as the primary cause of the collapse, and there would appear to be plenty of evidence that the Western world today is in grave danger of suffering the same fate and for the same reasons.

In J's parable, when Adam had got his partner, it seemed that everything in the garden was, quite literally, lovely. They both enjoyed a wonderful sense of happiness, innocence and contentment. But it was too good to last, as the writer was only too well aware. There is evil in this world and it had been there from the beginning. But where did it come from and how did it have such an effect? What could have corrupted such a promising start? J looks round for a creature to play the part of the spoiler in his parable, and what better than the serpent? It came slithering in, pretending to be Eve's friend and professing to have their interests at heart, but in actual fact plotting to bring about their downfall. Isn't that how temptation so often works? The writer of the First Letter of Peter (5.8) warned that 'The devil goes about like a roaring lion, seeking whom he may devour,' but he doesn't, at least not very often or obviously. If he did, it would be much easier to keep out of his way. Neither does he go about like a pantomime figure, dressed in black and with a forked tail and horns. If so, he would be the object of ridicule and contempt, rather than being treated with any kind of consideration. The tempter doesn't work like that. He is a master of disguise, ranging from a dinner-jacket to dungarees, and appearing far more often in the guise of a sympathizer than spoiler.

'Everything all right?' said the serpent to Eve, with a false façade of friendliness. 'Oh yes', she replied, 'We're both very happy and contented thank you.' But he persisted. 'Is there anything you *can't* do? Surely things aren't as perfect as all that are they? There must be something you would like to do, if you could.' 'Well, now you come to mention it,' said Eve, 'there is just one thing. That tree over there. We've been told that if we eat from that we shall die.' The serpent didn't bat an eyelid; nor would he even if he had possessed one. He didn't propose that he eat from the tree himself, just as an example. He was far cleverer than that. 'That really is nonsense, my dear,' he assured her. 'You want to be a little more adventurous. You are out of touch with modern, on-going ideas. You need to be a shade more sophisticated, more mature in your outlook. You have to live for the present sometimes, you know, and let the future look after itself. That fruit is obviously there to be eaten, not just admired, so try it. Rules are all right in their way, and rule-makers, for that matter, and I should be the first to admit it, but it's fun to please yourself – spoil yourself is the phrase I would use – a bit sometimes. Gets you out of the routine. After all, appetites are there to be satisfied, so if I were you I would risk it. There won't be any consequences or come-back.'

But of course, there were! Doing what we want to do doesn't always square with what we ought to do. J, with his finger so accurately on the pulse of human nature, plots the sequence step by step. When the two became conscious of their wrong-doing, they tried to hide away from God, but found that they couldn't. God had seen what had happened and wanted to know why. The happiness was over, the innocence was gone, and the sense of guilt and shame set in. Then came the attempts to shift the blame. Adam blamed Eve and, notice, he tried to blame God as well. 'The woman *you* gave me ... *she* tempted me.' 'It's your fault God, not mine.' Clever stuff, that. An exercise often indulged in by those whose moral muscles are flabby and they think this is short-cut to spiritual fitness. When things go well, God and his goodness are taken for granted, but when things go wrong, he is quickly blamed. 'What have I done to deserve this?' is the cry, and the implication is very often that somehow God has for some reason, inflicted it upon them. Eve, in her turn, blamed the snake, who found that he couldn't pass the buck back any further. The excuses were noisy, but that was because they were empty.

It all sounds so very up-to-date, which is how it should sound if the Bible is read as relevant for today. Our modern society seems to thrive on trying to shift the blame for everything that goes wrong on to someone or something else. Rejecting criticism and refusing to take blame is a very popular pastime. Criminals in courts, accused of all kinds of crimes, cry out against the circumstances of their upbringing and environment, the failure of the state, or sometimes the school, to appreciate their problems, and the way in which the world about them has forced them into follies not of their own making. The corporation, council, organization, or state industry, which 'Flatly rejects and repudiates all allegations' of their inefficiency, neglect, indifference or irresponsibility. The family quarrel, the bad debts, the bad temper, crime, cowardice, indulgence and selfishness, the taking advantage of another person's weakness or need, can have all alibis and excuses that may sound attractive and worthy, but which are really very hollow and cheap. Of course, we are all products, or some would say victims, of our environment, genetic inheritance, upbringing and early influences, but to point to these things as the recurring reasons for our failures, or even for our successes, is a refusal to face up to ourselves. In Jeremiah's day, people had perfected this idea of trying to blame others and had put it into a proverb. 'Our fathers have eaten sour grapes,' they said, 'so the children's teeth are set on edge' (Jer 31.29). The prophet poured scorn on this kind of escapism and reminds the people of their individual responsibilities.

So, in J's parable, came the consequences, for all the characters. The snake was suddenly seen in its true colours and nature, false, feared and often fatal, and both the man and the woman received their sentences. No doubt the writer is trying to explain certain simple, basic questions that often puzzled people in the ancient world, such as why snakes were so often seen as an 'accursed' part of creation, why women experienced pain in childbirth and why most men laboured all their lives for precious little, with an early death at the end of it, and so on. But in my view, one of the most important and profound truths which J is trying to portray is what one could call the Eternal Triangle of relationships. There is the relationship between the man and the woman – love, marriage, sexual relationships; the relationship of them both to the 'garden' – the environment, the world of Nature, the rest of creation; the relationship of them both to God –the obedience and response to his demands. Keep those contacts good, the writer is saying, and the sum total of the triangle, from every angle, will add up to happiness. But spoil and corrupt them, with your pornography and permissiveness, your pollution and poisoning, your profanity and your polytheism, and the end product will be hell.

Hit the nail right on the head, did 'J'. Not much of a scientist, but a superb psychologist and sociologist. He analyses the condition with the skill of a spiritual surgeon. He knew that if people are to be really human, and not mere robots, they must have freedom of choice, and that freedom would mean that they could choose to obey or rebel against the demands of God. It was an occupational hazard in making humans higher than animals and thereby giving them the ability to do what was right by choice, not merely by instinct, but it was a risk God had to take. It was the result of making humans unique. Certan instincts would remain strong, but 'doing what comes naturally' would be overlaid by a matter of morality. For example, in a ship-wreck the instinct of self-preservation and survival is very strong, but letting someone else have one's place in the lifeboat is a different dimension. This kind of choice gives a person character and personality, depending on how they use it. In the parable, it is a freedom to which God can speak, but to which temptation can also appeal. It was a freedom within a responsibility, otherwise the liberty would quickly turn to licence.

The writer may not have known much about the scientific laws which govern this planet, by which we all have to abide or suffer the consequences, but he knew a lot about the moral laws, which are equally important and binding, and which came in when humanity was created. If we break those laws, there is always a price to pay. This is not some kind of phobia arising from out of a fable, as Freud tended to proclaim, it is a fact of life. I read recently that the human body contains many hundreds of millions of cells, all of which have particular jobs to do and which normally they carry out perfectly. But should any of those cells become renegade and refuse to obey the rules, by pleasing themselves, as it were, what they did and not caring about the welfare of the rest of the body, the result would be chaos and the condition could become a cancer.

The supposition that if only people can be set free from the domination of desire for 'good or evil', and released from the obsession with 'sin' they will then bring in their own 'golden age' of goodwill and progress has taken some nasty knocks in this present century, and a critical look at the state of modern society does not inspire much confidence in such notions. To all but the ostracized, who profess to be above it, and the 'ostriches', who prefer not to notice, it is very obvious that 'The time is out of joint', as Shakespeare's Hamlet observed, and that there are sicknesses in our midst that will take more than 'quack' medicines to cure.

J ends the parable with the account of the banishment of Adam from the garden and the setting up of a guard to make sure he didn't get back in. Some have seen this, quite wrongly in my view, as a basis for a belief in what they term 'original sin', but surely the essential truth is that this story, and indeed the whole of the first eleven chapters of Genesis, form the prologue to the Bible, not the epilogue. Certainly, human-kind had blotted its copy-book and, as we shall see, the story of Noah and the Flood takes the idea a step further, but that was not the end of the matter by any means. Adam had been banished from the garden, but there was a way back into a good relationship with God. That is what the whole biblical drama of salvation is all about. The banishment was an alienation, but not a final separation from God. Humanity had rebelled against its Creator, but God will not let go and the rest of the Bible sets out the preparation and plan for salvation, which would come to its climax and culmination in the cross of Christ, the ultimate provision for human redemption and re-creation.

The opening chapters of the first book in the Bible tell of the alienation of men and women from God, through their own faults and folly, but the last book in the Bible, known as Revelation, has a wonderful word picture of Jesus standing at the door of the human heart and saying, 'Behold, I stand at the door and knock; if anyone hears my voice and opens the door, I will come in and eat with them.' In between those two books runs the recurring theme of reconciliation with God. This 'golden thread' weaves its way right through the Bible and includes such exquisite words as those of the unknown prophet of the Exile (Isa. 55.7), pleading with the wrong-doer to 'Forsake his ways and thoughts and return unto the Lord, who will have mercy upon him, and to our God, who will abundantly pardon,' and the breathtaking vision of the psalmist (Ps. 139.9–10), 'If I take the wings of the morning and dwell in the uttermost parts of the sea, even there shall thou lead me and thy right hand shall hold me,' and, of course, the incomparable parable of the Prodigal Son (Luke 15).

In many modern minds, these Creation stories are often stored in some kind of mental 'attic', which is all too rarely visited, if at all. To go there, however, can be a useful and rewarding experience, providing one remembers that in order to let some light into what may well be cob-webbed corners, it is vital to remember that great poems and parables can act as windows, through which light can come and through which further views and truths should be seen.

2

Noah and the Flood

> And the animals all went in two by two,
> But I don't believe it. What about you?

That is a little rhyme which reflects the attitude of many
people towards the story of Noah's ark and the Flood – one of
bantering and bathos. To the majority of people, such a story
can safely be consigned to the realms of fantasy, or legend, or
myth, or whatever kind of mental dustbin they may decide
upon. Such tales, they say, are good fun for play-acting or
modern musicals, but taking them seriously is quite another
matter. Old Noah is all right for the very young, but when
one grows up, one puts away such childish things. In fact the
very idea of an old man building a gigantic box which housed
all those animals and finally came to rest on Ararat, or
'Araroot', as one boy once informed me, just about takes the
biscuit!

One would certainly go along with those sentiments except
for one thing – namely that there *was* a flood. Not of course,
on the world-wide scale and proportion as some imagine, for
the simple reason that when the Bible writers talk about 'all
the world', it is obvious that they could only mean 'the world'
as they knew it, which was a small part of the Ancient Near
and Middle East. Nevertheless, the Flood is now seen to be
based much more on fact than fiction or fable, though the

Bible writer's interpretation of why it happened is very much a matter of theological debate.

Not so very long ago, few but the most fanatical fundamentalists would have regarded the Flood story in Genesis chapters six to eight as anything more than flights of fancy, with no place among matters of fact, even though it was known that the story was not exclusive to the Bible. Just as stories of Creation are to be found in biblical and Babylonian accounts, as well as in the folk stories of most ancient civilizations, so the story of a flood are found in the folklore of places like India, Persia and Sumer, but it seemed impossible to pin any of them down to any one particular event.

Yet such legends had to have a beginning somewhere and scholars offered various theories as to their origins. Some said they were variations of Creation stories, when the earth was said to have been all covered with water and then land emerged out of the waters. Others said they had grown out of some definite disaster which had left such an impression on ancient people that they had enshrined it in their folk stories and imaginations, giving them all the inevitable variations and 'embroideries' as the stories were told and re-told over the years. That would account for the way they were adapted to suit particular backgrounds and beliefs.

The idea of a 'local' disaster seemed the most probable, yet there was no definite evidence which would lift it out of the 'legend' category into the realm of reasonable acceptance. Not until, that is, archaeology took a hand and began to show that some 'myths' at least, had some roots in reality. Henry C. Rawlinson, excavating at the site of ancient Nineveh, at the turn of the century, unearthed some large clay tablets, twelve in all, and on one of them, when they were deciphered, the eleventh to be exact, was found another version of a flood disaster. The significance of this find, however, was that this was not just another variation. This Babylonian version, dating from about 1700 BC, so closely resembled the biblical account that the coincidence could not be accidental. Either one had copied from the other or they were both based on a common source.

But the question still remained. Had there ever been an actual flood or were the stories all the figment of fertile folklore imagination? The answer came about thirty years after the cuneiform writing on Rawlinson's tablets, now known as the 'Gilgamesh Epic', had been deciphered. This had shown that the original authors of the tablets were not Babylonian, but Sumerian, a much older race, whose capital had been at Ur, in Chaldea, from where Abraham's family was said to have started (Gen.11.31). In 1923, Sir Leonard Wooley, the British Archaeologist, began to dig at Tell Mugayyar, near the Persian Gulf and believed to be the site of ancient Ur. In one of the mounds he found the 'Royal Cemetery' and the lowest part of these tombs produced evidence of a settlement at around 3000 BC. After that, there were no more signs of habitation, but neither was it virgin soil. It was clay. On an impulse, Wooley dug down through the clay, about three metres thick, and underneath found fresh evidence of human settlement. Obviously some tremendous inundation had overwhelmed the earlier civilization and later communities had built on top of the clay. Stephen Langdon, excavating near to ancient Babylon, at Kish, found similar deposits, though far less thick and possibly not from the same period.

The evidence seemed conclusive and in 1929 Wooley sent his cryptic message to a startled world – 'We have found the flood.' Actually, perhaps it should have read 'We have found *a* flood,' because there was not sufficient evidence to equate the discoveries with the Genesis story. The archaeologists had only proved that certain civilizations had been interrupted, at different periods and in different places, by floods of considerable and unusual magnitude, though how such a deluge had happened was impossible to say. They gave a date for the earliest period of the disaster of about 4000 BC.

Some people, both then and since, have been guilty of drawing conclusions from all this which are not valid. They have assumed that archaeology can 'prove' certain bibilical events to be true and that there is little else to be said. It is certainly true that archaeology can light up the narratives at

many points and can help tremendously in our understanding of the background to various events. It is also true that
there must be a great deal waiting to be discovered and some
of it will no doubt shed light on some of the biblical stories, if
and when such discoveries are made.

But it would be foolish to overestimate what archaeology
can do, or has done in this direction, because the truth of
many of the biblical stories and events rests on more than
a diligent digging up of the past. It is the story of God's
dealing with mankind and that is a field and a sphere in
which scientific investigation, including archaeology, has to
proceed with care. What it can do, in a very wonderful way,
is to provide information and knowledge that is invaluable
towards our understanding of what some of these stories
are trying to teach us. Archaeology is concerned mainly
with remains of human activity and struggle for survival.
This sometimes follows similar patterns but because human
beings do not always behave consistently, or follow a particular pattern of behaviour, conclusions have to be drawn
with caution. Therefore, although Wooley proved that some
ancient people living at the top of the Persian Gulf were
once overwhelmed by a great deal of water, it is no use
pretending that this proved the whole of the Flood story to
be true.

It would appear that the ancient story was carried into
Canaan, long before the Israelites lived there, and then
became part of their cultural tradition when they later came
to settle in Canaan – their 'Promised Land' – after the Exodus
from Egypt. Therefore similarities in the Gilgamesh and
Genesis stories are to be expected and they are obvious when
the accounts are compared. The Babylonian tablet tells how
the gods decided to send a flood on the earth, but one of
them, Ea, had the foresight to forewarn his favourite mortal,
Utnapishtim, of what was about to happen. He told the
mortal to build a boat of definite proportions, which meant it
was shorter than Noah's construction, but quite a bit wider,
and take on board his family and some animals, though not as
many as Noah. Utnapishtim himself said 'I made it up with all

22

I had of silver and gold.' Evidently he was putting a little by for a rainy day!

Then the storm 'marched across the heavens, turning all light into darkness' and raged for six days and nights. On the seventh day Utnapishtim sent out a dove and a swallow, both of which came back, then a raven, which did not. Then, as the boat came to rest on Mount Nizir, said to be in Assyria, he opened the hatchway and as the light fell on his face he fell on his knees and wept. Afterwards the flood subsided and he offered sacrifices to the gods for his safe survival. The gods, apparently, 'smelled the fragrance and gathered like flies round the sacrifice', with no doubt each one eager for his share.

The main things to notice, however, are not the similarities between the Babylonian and biblical accounts, startling as they are, but the differences. The Bible account, which most scholars consider to be a combinaton of the J and P sources, actually says (Gen. 8.14), that the ark came to rest on the *mountains* of Ararat, which surely indicates a mountainous area, not a particular peak. In the Second Book of Kings (19.37), when the sons of Sennacherib, the Assyrian king, slew their father, it says they 'escaped into the land of Ararat', which was then the Assyrian Urartu, but which is now the territory of Armenia, between Turkey and Iran, and in the USSR. In that area the highest peak by far is known as 'Aghri Dagh', which in Turkish means 'painful Mountain' ... probably because it is so difficult to climb. This peak has long been known as Mount Ararat.

Most of the world's very high mountains are surrounded by lower peaks, which often impair the mountain's view and impact, but of Ararat's 17,000 feet, almost 14,000 feet towers above flat base plains, making it the world's longest such uninterrupted slope. Such majesty demands reverence and respect, and it is not very surprising that this lofty, lonely peak has long assumed the reputation as the place where Noah's ark came to rest. But despite numerous expeditions there, ever since 1829, when a German professor and explorer proved that the mountain was not impossibly high nor impossibly holy, by climbing to the top, as well as lots of claims for all kinds of sightings, no really tangible evidence for the existence of the ark has so far been found. A piece of fossilized wood brought down by a Frenchman in 1955 was first thought to be about 5,000 years old, but has since been radiocarbon-dated at only about 1,400 years of age. No one claims that this kind of dating is completely infallible, but since its inception and invention, in 1949, by W. F. Libby, it has proved to be a very reliable method of ascertaining the age of fossil material, and there seems little reason to doubt its accuracy in this case.

Claims by certain expeditions and war-time aircraft pilots to have taken photographs of strange box-like objects on the mountain side have not proved conclusive and as yet it should be said that no firm evidence has been found. Moreover, in recent years all ark-hunting attempts have been halted ... probably because the area lies too near very secret and sensitive military zones! All that, however, is, in my view, beside the point. The real value of the stories does not lie in the location of Ararat or the finding of the ark, but in trying to define and discover what the stories meant and what the writers were really trying to tell us. Even if one day the remains of the ark should be found, if the significance of the stories has been lost, the writers' purpose will not have been realized. That is why the differences between the biblical and Babylonian accounts, or any other folk-stories about great floods, are far more important than the similarities. In the Babylonian story, the reason for the flood was given as the capriciousness and cruelty of the gods, who seemed to take a delight in destruction and cruelty for their own sakes, but the biblical account has a very different interpretation.

The story begins (Gen. 6.5) by saying that when God saw all the evil being committed all over the earth by human beings, he was sorry that he had ever made them at all. Some versions state that 'God knew that the thoughts and inclinations of everyone were evil all the time, and he was sorry he had ever made them and put them upon the earth.' The word used for 'inclination', or 'imagination', was the Hebrew word 'yezer' and it had great significance in Jewish thought. It meant 'mind', or 'impulse', and it described the good and evil tendencies in the human heart. God had created human beings for a fullness of life ... life in communion with their creator and with one another. But now evil of every kind was widespread, with people in revolt against God and determined to indulge in corruption and violence of every description. Human culture had got off to a very bad start. There was, apparently, progress in the arts and advancement in what we might call technology, for in Gen. 21–22 we read of 'Jubal, who was the ancestor of those who play the harp and pipe', and of 'Tubal-cain, the master of all blacksmiths and coppersmiths'. But such progress had been accompanied by greed and immorality, and a chain reaction of evil had set in, which mocked and marred the apparent advancements.

In the writer's view, there is one thing left for God to do. Humanity had left him no choice. There had to be a judgement, even though it was to be tempered with concern and sorrow ... The Lord 'Was sorry he had made them and it grieved him to his heart', but he came to the conclusion that the only solution was to erase all life from the earth, go back to the drawing-board, as it were, and begin all over again. Here we see the writer's interpretation of the reason for the flood. It was a judgment and a punishment for sin and evil. That is why he is not concerned about how it happened, for he offers no explanation of that, but why it happened. It was not just a divine malicious whim, it was the action of a righteous God who had seen human beings become so corrupt and had polluted the earth to such an extent, throwing back in God's face with contempt all the ideas of goodness and responsibility he had given them, that a clean sweep was the only way to remove all the stains.

This was the only way the writer, or at least the J writer, could work it out, for this introduction to the Flood story came from that source. There had to be a reason for the catastrophe and since in his view all things came from God, the reason had to have a moral consideration. Later on, in Gen. 19.24, we see the same idea again, when 'The Lord rained down fire and brimstone upon Sodom and Gomorrah' because the people there were 'exceedingly wicked'. But as we read these reasons for the disasters, we can surely sense shortcomings in them. We can go along with the writer's observation that material advancement had not been matched by moral progress. The latter half of this twentieth century has seen technological achievements and discoveries that to many have been miraculous, but side-by-side with the development has come a spread of brutality and bloodshed on a scale that reminds others more of a dark age than a golden age. But as for the assumption that people and places are visited by disasters as a punishment for sin, if that were true why stop at Sodom? There are plenty of other places in the world which, if that criterion were applied, should receive the same treatment, but they seem to remain unscathed. Also, if floods, or famines, or earthquakes, or hurricanes are to be seen as a punishment for sins, are we to see the people who suffer such disasters as deserving the fate because of their evil ways?

We know, of course, that earthquakes and volcanoes, for example, are all part of the continuing process of creation and that therefore we live on certain parts of this planet at our own risk, as it were. Also, it is becoming increasingly obvious that human error, greed and indifference play their part in making matters much worse. One cannot divorce some of the floods in Asia, for example, from foolish deforestation, or some of the famine in Africa from cruel civil wars, and perhaps freak weather conditions in many parts of the world from the pollution of the atmosphere and the punching of holes in the ozone layer. When we treat nature like that, it tends to hit back hard. But to brandish a Bible at the victims of these disasters, many of whom are very poor and very young, and who have often lost everything they possessed, and tell them that their suffering has been visited upon them as some kind of divine retribution for their shortcomings, would border on the blasphemous. Yet such reasoning is found in more than a few minds and in Luke's Gospel (13.1–5); Jesus had to contend with such suppositions, but he made his views on such ideas very clear.

Indeed, before the flood story is finished, the writer himself realizes, or at least the J source does, that disasters do not have the last word and that God has other plans for humanity's salvation, but in the meantime he presses on with the story, telling how in the midst of all the general revolt against God, one man 'found favour in the eyes of the Lord'. His name was Noah, which probably meant 'Rest', or 'Quiet', and he is described as a very good man, in fact a faultless figure, who 'walked with God'. Because of this goodness, he is singled out for salvation from the coming disaster and was told to build a boat, or rather a huge box-like structure, measuring about 133 metres long, 22 metres wide and 13 metres high, and having three stories. That is about half the length and breadth of the QE 2, and one wonders where Noah got all the materials and who helped him to build it, since there is no mention of anyone else being at all interested in what the old man was doing!

But Noah built in faith, even though he must have been bewildered by the whole thing. In the entire story, although there is a lot about what Noah did, there is no mention of anything he actually said. He just did as he was told, without comment or criticism. This is very different from the Babylonian version, where Utnapishtim is not only 'in' on the whole thing, but also his being saved was pure selfishness. It was nothing to do with him being 'righteous', but rather of being 'all right' and not bothering in the least what happened to everyone else. To be sure, in the biblical account there are naive, anthropomorphic touches in the story, like God actually closing the door of the ark when he had seen everybody in, but this does not distract from the main point. The one God, in contrast to the many Babylonian deities, had acted to accomplish his purpose, but a righteous 'remnant' would survive and be able to make a new beginning.

Both accounts say the flood was divinely ordained, but whereas the Gilgamesh story says the gods were in confusion and chaos, the Genesis account tells of the one God who was in complete control. The Babylonian tablet tells us that the disaster was dictated by mere caprice and spite on the part of the gods, and then afterwards they all tried to disclaim any responsibility for it. In fact, they all blame one another and are in utter disagreement over the necessity for the flood or the justice of it. Also, the catastrophe was intended for all and sundry, good and evil alike without exception. If Ea, one of the gods, had not intervened to save his favourite mortal, all mankind would have perished without compunction or compassion. In the biblical account, Noah was spared not because of a whim but because he had 'walked with God'. The Babylonian version shows a crude polytheism, with the gods crouching in fear when the storm was raging and then swarming like flies in a frenzy when the flood was finished. This is poles apart from the dignity and monotheism of the biblical account, in which one God, the creator and controller of all things, rules and over-rules to achieve his purpose.

The main difference, however, is the covenant which concludes the biblical story. This idea of a covenant runs right through the Bible and since the second century AD it has been seen in the Christian church as consisting of two covenants, one based on the covenant with Moses at Sinai (Ex. 19), and the other on the life and death of Jesus, which was the 'New Covenant in his blood' (Mark 14.24). The Hebrew word for covenant, 'berith', was translated in the Latin Vulgate as 'Testamentum', from which we get the word 'testament', so we speak of the 'Old Testament' and the 'New Testament'. This idea of a covenant signifies a peculiar and particular relationship between God and human beings, which brings the two together, even though a covenant was an agreement between two unrelated parties. Therefore it was of the 'Lord's mercy' that he was willing to bind himself to people in a covenant he would never break.

Before the promise is made to Noah, 'God thinks it to himself' (8.21), and then decides that never again will he 'Put the earth under a curse because of what humans do', and then makes the promise 'As long as the earth remains, seedtime and harvest, cold and heat, summer and winter, day and night, shall not cease' (8.22). It is as though the writer, having first given his reasons for why the flood was sent, as a punishment for evil, now looks round at the world in which he himself lives and realizes that if punishment had been the purpose, it had failed. The evil was still very much in evidence and there seemed precious little sign of much improvement as far as sinfulness was concerned. If the flood had been sent to teach people a lesson, it had not succeeded.

Therefore the writer comes to the conclusion that if people are to be brought into a right relationship with God, the real answer was by co-operation not catastrophe. With this conclusion, the writer climbs to a theological mountain-top. He opens a window and looks a long way ahead to the lengths to which God will go to redeem mankind. Not only does he see God as the God who controls the crops and the seasons – seedtime and harvest – which in those days was seen by most to be in control of the Baals, the spirit and agricultural gods, but also he sees the kind of harvest which co-operation with God could produce. If Man would realize that he is not the owner of the earth, but just the trustee and caretaker, there would be the benefits of such collaboration in so many fields of human endeavour.

The biblical writer also touches on another truth which is not found in the Gilgamesh Epic. This is that the orderliness and dependability of the seasons is just as much a manifestation of God's power as was the destruction of the flood. In those days it was far easier and much more customary to see the hand of God in the majestic and the violent – 'the wind, the earthquake and the fire' – rather than in the quiet pattern of seedtime and harvest. It was more usual to expect God to act in the dramatic than in the ordinary, daily routine. But the writer sees God being involved in all aspects of life, not just in the sensational. God was to do with the mundane as well as with the mountain-tops of life.

In all this, however, there is a warning. The development from seedtime to a good harvest is not a foregone conclusion. Both in nature and in human nature, poor sowing and careless cultivation, as well as outside influences, can result in the whole rhythm being spoilt. Even good seed cannot be guaranteed to fulfil the promise and potential it first possessed. The

29

---

writer drives home this point in his sad sequel which ends the flood story. He describes how the covenant with Noah is sealed by the sign of the rainbow in the sky. The actual words are, 'I will set my bow in the clouds and it shall be a sign of the covenant between me and the earth.' Probably the writer was thinking of the bow as a weapon, as in Ps. 7.12–13, rather than a refraction or reflection of light on the raindrops, but the meaning is the same. The bow was both a sign that the storm was over and that the power and promises of God are in evidence. Perhaps the 'bow in the clouds' meant that God's 'weapon' was now shrouded and would not be used again against man.

Then came the sad ending and the writer's reminder that even a man as good as Noah can degenerate. After the flood, and presumably after the waters had subsided sufficiently, Noah settled down to be a farmer, tilling the soil and planting a vineyard. From the grapes he made wine and drank himself into a drunken stupor. Then he lay in his tent naked and obnoxious. The man who had personified integrity and persevered in goodness was now a pitiable and pathetic spectacle, lacking the kind of self-discipline and self-respect which had been the hall-mark of his personality. The one who had responded so definitely to the time of crisis now behaved so differently when the danger was past. The man who had stood so upright on the ark now lay on the land as an object of pity and contempt.

One could say, of course, that what Noah did in the privacy of his own tent was his own business and that he was entitled to a bit of relaxation now the tension was over. Or perhaps that he wanted to indulge in a desire to escape from the pressures upon him, or possibly what had started out as a harmless whim had got tragically out of hand. Perhaps he thought that what he did now the danger was past was not very important and in any case it would have no ill-effects either on himself or anyone else. But such comparisons are risky, as the writer makes clear. One of Noah's sons, Ham, sees his father lying naked in the tent and, no doubt in some distress, goes to tell his two brothers, Shem and Japheth.

They decide to do what seems to be the decent thing, which was to take a coat of some kind and cover their father with it. The story says they walked backwards in order to do this, with the garment held between them. They obviously didn't want their father to think they had even seen him in that state.

All this was bad enough, but then, when Noah woke up his anger was directed not against himself, but against the son who had first seen him in that state. In the only words he utters in the whole story, he curses Ham or rather 'Canaan', one of Ham's sons. Since later tradition said that the three sons of Noah represented the ancestors of the main races of the ancient world, with Ham the 'father' of the people of Ethiopia, Egypt and Canaan, some see in this incident a reason or excuse, for racial prejudice. They point out that Noah said Canaan would be 'slave of slaves to his brothers', so they see support for regarding certain races as inferior.

This kind of 'interpretation' is a good example of the game some people play, in 'finding' texts in the bible to justify particular attitudes or points of view. The writer was obviously referring to, and reflecting the later hatred that developed between the Israelites and the Canaanites when the Israelites entered Canaan – their 'Promised Land'. Noah's drunkeness was symbolic of the kind of debauchery and immorality found in some of the Canaanite religious festivals, when an over-indulgence in wine and the worship of the 'fertility' gods often resulted in shameful excesses. When Noah cried out, 'Cursed be Canaan', it was bitter reaction and condemnation of the kind of temptations the Israelites faced in Canaan and to which many of them, as the future was to show, succumbed. To try to use such texts, as do certain sections of the Dutch Reformed Church in South Africa, as well as some sects of the Christian Church in America, to justify their discrimination against coloured people, is to be guilty of writing their own scriptures and forging God's signature to them. One can find texts in the Bible to condone or condemn almost anything, but it mustn't mean wrenching the words out of the original context and making them mean other than they were intended.

31

The story ends by telling how Noah lived on after the flood for another 350 years and died at the ripe old age of 950! What he did in his remaining years is not stated. The flood had been his 'limelight' and the rest of his life was spent in the shadows. He gets a mention in various other books of the Bible, in Isa. 54.4 and Ezek. 14.14, for example, and in Matt. 24.37 where Jesus compared the days of Noah to the 'coming of the Son of Man'. Possibly he meant that just as people in Noah's time took precious little notice of all the warning signs before the flood and ignored the danger of coming disaster, so people of every age imagine that whatever evils they do, there will be no consequences or comeback. Whatever we may believe about Noah and his ark, it would be very foolish to dismiss the story as something that has no relevance for today. We may no longer see disasters as signs of God's attitude towards evil, at least natural disasters, but revolt against God's rules will always bring some kind of reckoning and retribution. The floods of violence, immorality and hatred will inevitably break down the dams of human decency and dignity, and opening the floodgates of greed and selfishness, and a pandering to the lowest common denominators in life, instead of encouraging the highest common factors, will always lead to an aftermath of bitterness and suffering. It is a fact of life.

As theology, the flood story may sound childlike, but it is not childish. There is wisdom in it, just as in the pictures that children draw, and there is a realization that human sins are such that only a God of supreme love and compassion can cope with it. That is why the writer bids us remember the rainbow, the sign and symbol of God's mercy towards humanity. It was not just a token covenant, or an 'interim' one until a more permanent one can be made. It is an everlasting covenant, a guarantee of eternal goodness, a merciful love to all people, reaching its final revelation in the New Covenant of Jesus the Messiah.

3

Moses and the Burning Bush

Moses in the bullrushes, Moses in the cradle,
Moses and the Burning Bush ... believe *that*, if you are able!

Not great poetry, by any stretch of the imagination, but
enough doggerel to describe how lots of people view the main
events in the life of Moses, or at least what they see as the
main events, and certainly those which lend themselves to
the most scepticism.

In actual fact, the writer of these events, in Ex. 1–4, is very
vague about dates and ages, being satisfied with phrases such
as 'During this time', or 'Years passed', or 'One day, when
Moses was grown up'. Later tellers of the stories, however, as
can be seen in Stephen's speech in Acts 6, tended to divide
Moses' life up into three periods of forty years each, though,
of course the phrase 'forty years' in the Old Testament, could
mean many things. The first period was concerned with his
birth and early life in Egypt, the second covered his 'exile' in
the land of Midian, and the third told of his return to Egypt
to rescue the slaves with the subsequent journey through the
wilderness to the Promised Land.

Finally, according to Deut. 34.7, having delivered the
Israelites to within sight of Canaan, Moses died at the ripe old
age of 120 (which is three times forty), 'when his sight was still
not dimmed nor his strength diminished'. It was during the

'middle' period of his life that he had the encounter with the bushfire 'on the west side of the wilderness', near to Sinai, or Horeb, the 'holy mountain'. One notes that by the time of Moses, the enthusiasm of the Bible writers for giving their heroes great ages had mellowed quite a lot, from the heady days of Methuselah's 969 years, Noah's 950 and Lamech's 777! Exactly why they indulged in this kind of age 'inflation' is not quite clear, although there are many interesting theories put forward, ranging from a great veneration for old age and long life which may have resulted in many years being added in order to make that particular life more noticeable, to the possibility that many generations were omitted from the 'family trees' and the missing years were then condensed and credited to the one person.

Whatever the reason, it is important to note that these great ages are found only in the opening chapters of the book of Genesis ... in the 'pre-history' period, and that from Genesis 12 onwards there is a 'sliding scale', with Abraham's father down to a mere 275, Abraham himself to 175, Moses to 120 and so on down to David, who lived only to a very modest ... and realistic ... seventy! Perhaps, as time went on, the Chroniclers learnt to record events more accurately, or perhaps to count time more correctly. Another possibility, of course, is that later writers wanted the readers to judge characters more by actions than by ages!

However, even if we take the view, as many do, that each 'forty years' of 'Moses' life really represented a generation rather than a known number, with a generation being about twenty-five years, it still means that he was about fifty when he saw a bush 'which was aflame yet not reduced to ashes'. But much more important than his age, or the location where it happened ... for there are lots of arguments as to where Sinai, or Horeb, or 'the holy mountain', or 'The Mountain of God', whichever translation one prefers, is actually to be found ... is what exactly we are being asked to believe about it all. A bush setting on fire in the tinder-dry Sinai wilderness would not have been uncommon by any means, but when it says that the bush was on fire but was not burnt up and then a voice was heard calling out of the middle of the flames, what can we make of that?

The best approach, I believe, is to look first at the whole background to the 'burning bush' incident. To do that, we must let the camera, as it were, 'pan away' from that tiny spot and take an aerial, if not a satellite view of the ancient world of the Near and Middle East at that particular time, which was, so many scholars believe, about 1300 BC. More than 400 years before that, the Israelites had found, or maybe forced their way into Egypt, or rather into the area of the delta of the Nile known as Goshen, probably in the wake of an invasion of Egypt by the 'Hyksos' tribes, which occurred about 1720 BC. These fierce conquerors ... 'rulers of foreign countries', as the Egyptian word means ... dominated Egypt for almost 200 years, until about 1550 BC, when Ahmoses overthrew them and restored the rule of the Pharaohs.

All this fits in well with the stories in Gen. 39–50, of Joseph being sold into slavery in Egypt, making good, becoming prime minister and then sending for his family to come down from Canaan and settle in Goshen. This would explain the migration of the Israelites into Goshen and is really the 'prelude' to the Exodus, for if there had been no migration there would have been no slavery and no eventual rescue. Therefore, the Genesis stories set the scene for what later Hebrews regarded as the greatest event in their history ... being brought out of slavery by God and therefore being chosen for a particular purpose in the world. To date this 'coming out', as the Greek word 'Exodus' means, is the subject of much discussion among scholars, but many have come to the conclusion that the Pharaoh who forgot all that Joseph had done for Egypt, in safeguarding the harvests and apparently putting Egypt in a strong economic position, was Seti I, (1319–1301 BC), and the Pharaoh who was in power during the actual Exodus was Rameses II, who ruled from *c.* 1290–1224 BC. Ex. 12.40 says that the people of Israel had been in Egypt for 430 years and if that refers to the whole time, not just to the slavery, it would fit in well with the time of the Hyksos invasion (1290 + 430 = 1720).

All this is very much conjecture, since the Bible writers are not very forthcoming with their historical dates and in any case, the stories of the Exodus were not actually written down for hundreds of years after the events, being handed on orally for many generations, and no doubt getting more and more 'embroidered' as they were told. Therefore, scholars talk about the 'traditions' and 'legends' associated with the Exodus stories, and examiners set questions which begin, 'Despite the presence of legend, in the narratives'. There seems little doubt that we are dealing with stories which are difficult to define and for which there is a dearth of actual documentary evidence to 'prove' them true. Furthermore, although the Exodus was of paramount importance to the Israelites, there is no mention of it at all in any Egyptian documents. Perhaps the escape of a few slaves was seen as of no special significance, or possibly the Egyptians were not too keen on reporting their failure to re-capture them, but whatever the reason, Egyptian records are strangely silent on the subject.

Nevertheless, even if we allow for all the omissions and exaggerations, as we must, we are still left with a man, in Moses, who must surely rank with the greatest leaders and lawgivers the world has ever known. For a man who could take a rabble of slaves away from what was to many of them the comparative safety of slavery, because they said to him more than once, 'If only we had died in Egypt, where we sat round the flesh-pots and had plenty of bread to eat', to trek across hundreds of miles of wilderness to a 'Promised Land', must have been a remarkable person by any standards. Although he never entered the land himself, he delivered the slaves, by then disciplined and determined, to its borders, and despite the difficulties, distances and determination of some scholars to dismiss the stories as products of popular imagination, one must see Moses as a man of tremendous courage and patience, willing to give himself utterly in the service of his people and to atone for their sins by offering to suffer on their behalf. Some see in this an 'anticipation' of the life of Jesus and there is no doubt that Moses deserved the epitaph which the writer gives him ... 'There has never arisen in Israel a prophet like Moses, whom the Lord knew face to face' (Deut. 34.10).

However, to go back to the beginning, we first meet Moses as a 'baby in the bullrushes' when the ill-treatment of the new Pharaoh had just begun. Whatever the actual date of his birth, there is no doubt that he was born at a time of great crisis for the Hebrews. The delta of the Nile, where they had settled, was strategically very important and since, according to Ex. 1.7, they had 'increased in numbers and become very powerful', it was evident that they had become more of a political force than an economic asset, as far as the Egyptians were concerned. No doubt the Pharaohs had let them live there as long as they caused no trouble and certainly they had been a very useful source of cheap labour, but now the new king looked at them with some suspicion. He wondered whether, in the event of an enemy invading Egypt, either from land or sea, the Hebrews in Goshen would fight for the invaders or for the Egyptians. He decided to play safe and take no chances, so he embarked upon attempts to wipe them out, or at least so drastically reduce their numbers that they would be in no fit state to fight anybody!

First, he subjected them to harsh slavery and hard labour, building store cities such as Pithom and Ramases, but, as the writer triumphantly tells it, 'The more harshly they were treated, the more they multiplied'. The Pharaoh then ordered the midwives to kill all the baby boys at birth, though only two midwives didn't seem many for all the Israelites, but that failed too, so the 'final solution' was to order his soldiers to throw every Hebrew baby boy into the Nile. Many must have perished, but Moses survived, by a combination of connivance and craftiness, not to mention a liberal helping of colourful imagination on the part of the story-teller! He was said to have been hidden in an 'ark', or 'box', made from woven reeds, and then floated down the Nile just at a time and place to conveniently catch the attention of an Egyptian princess, who happened to like bathing there. Some scholars regard this 'Moses in the bullrushes' story as a folk story concocted to give him a 'special' start in life and it is certainly just the kind of tale that would have delighted Eastern audiences. Also, of course, it is very similar to the story of Sargon of Akkad (*c.* 2300 BC) being rescued from rushes on the river Euphrates in the same way and growing up to be king of Agade.

The fact remains, however, when we divide the fact from the fiction, that Moses must have been separated from slavery and trained for leadership at an early age. Certainly his name comes from a play on words, from the Hebrew 'Mosheh', meaning 'to draw from', and an Egyptian word meaning 'to give birth'. It is also obvious that he must have had the kind of education and training in arts, magical crafts and 'miracle working' usually found in Egyptian high circles, so the notion of him being brought up as an Egyptian prince is not so far-fetched.

However, despite his adoption and upbringing by the Pharaoh's daughter, Moses never lost sight of the fact that he was, by birth, a Hebrew, though if the story of his mother being able to act as his nurse is authentic (Ex. 2.9), she must take most credit for this. In fact, he apparently felt so strongly about his Hebrew ancestry that it eventually became the reason why he had to leave Egypt so suddenly. 'When he was grown up' ... there is no mention of his childhood or youth ... he saw an Egyptian slave-driver ill-treating a Hebrew slave and he was so incensed by the brutality that he killed the Egyptian and hid the body in the sand. Attempts are sometimes made to minimize this and excuse Moses by saying that he didn't really intend to kill the man and that it was accidental, but the writer makes it quite clear ... 'He looked round and when he saw that no one was watching, he killed the man' (Ex.2.12).

Moses may have thought that was the end of the matter, but the next day, when he tried to part two Hebrews who were fighting each other, one rounded on him with the words, 'Do you intend to kill me like you killed that Egyptian?' Realizing that the game was up, Moses made a hasty getaway to the land of Midian, probably in the eastern part of the Sinai Peninsula.

Soon afterwards, he was involved in yet another rescue act, this time helping a group of girls who were trying to water their father's sheep at a well but were being molested by some rather uncouth shepherds. Moses seemed to be making a habit of taking the part of the oppressed, but it was certainly symbolic of his later role in life. It is interesting to note that the girls assumed that he was an Egyptian, for when they told their father, Jethro, about it, they said, 'An Egyptian helped us'. He must have looked and spoken like one, but all these interventions show his anger at the sight of ill-treatment and his impulse to help those in need, and any attempt to analyse his character and assess his qualities of leadership should bear this in mind.

However, his chivalry towards the shepherd girls seems to have paid dividends better than his other rescue operations, for he was soon invited to supper at Jethro's house and in no time had married one of Jethro's daughters, Zipporah. If one wished to be a little sceptical, one could say that since Jethro had seven daughters, he was probably very pleased to get one of them married off and so possibly pushed the proposal, but as far as Moses was concerned, it was just the kind of security he was looking for. He soon settled down as a shepherd and when eventually his wife presented him with a baby son, his life seemed to have assumed a very quiet and peaceful pattern, with Egypt and all its problems left far behind.

Which is where the 'burning bush' comes into the story. The life of a shepherd in the Sinai Steppes was a lonely one and Moses had ample time, and food for thought. He had heard that the Pharaoh whom he had known in Egypt had died and that the new one was indulging in even harsher treatment of the Hebrew slaves. All this would no doubt be in Moses' mind as he sat with his sheep, but also no doubt he had calmed his conscience by convincing himself that although the Israelites were in great need, there was very little he could do to help them. Yet such thoughts would almost certainly be tempered by the realization that he had run away from his responsibilities. He had intended to retire from active service, as far as the slaves were concerned. He was very sorry for them and probably prayed about their plight, but he had a home and family to care for and a flock of sheep to look after, so how could he help them? His commitments were now his concern and the card he had hung on the door of his life said, in effect, 'Do not disturb'.

It was just at that point, however, that God *did* 'disturb' him, interrupting his whole life and thought. As Moses sat and soliloquized in the hot Sinai sun, he saw a bush 'which was on fire yet not burnt up'. 'This is strange', he thought, 'I will go closer and see.' So began his real encounter with the 'God of the fathers' and the challenge to him to stop just wondering about the slaves and to start working on ways to help them. It was going to be the opportunity for his 'rescue' acts to become reality in a way he had never dreamed of. The story is a masterpiece of Old Testament writing and to try and reduce it to the literal level is as foolish as trying to explain why the bush was not reduced to ashes. It is superb picture language and should be read in the same spirit as it was written, with great imagination and empathy. Trying to describe the indescribable is always difficult and great writers, both biblical and non-biblical, often resort to the technique of using symbolism and sign language.

Once Moses' attention had been attracted by the 'burning', the phenomenon is forgotten and is not mentioned again in the story. It may well have been that the sun's rays suddenly shone on the vivid colours of an acacia bush, which would then, in poetic parlance, 'seem to be aflame with fire'. Or perhaps the red sand was swept up around the bush by a whirlwind, which would look like smoke and fire ascending. There are lots of possibilities, but that is not the point. There is little doubt that Moses saw something unusual which made him turn aside to investigate, but a 'burning bush' is simply picture language. In the Old Testament, fire is often used as a symbol of God's presence and 'appearance' to people. It was the religious 'sign' of divine manifestation and Moses responded to it with interest. Whatever it was that he saw, it was translated and transfigured into a religious experience, during which time he was rooted to the spot with awe and wonder.

Moses and the Burning Bush

A moment later, the 'fire' had moved on and the bush was back to 'normal'. A lesser man than Moses might well have moved on too, shaking his head and rubbing his eyes, but not worrying any more about it. But Moses was not only awed, he was receptive. He was a seeker as well as a sight-seer. He realized that he was in the presence of divine power and reverence demanded that he take off his shoes, for this must be 'holy ground'. Then he heard a voice which called his name and made him aware that it was the 'God of the fathers' who was speaking to him. Moses 'hid his face' – probably buried his head in his hands – overcome by fear, 'afraid to gaze on God'. The voice told him that God had a plan and that Moses had a place in it. The plan was no less than the rescue of the slaves from Egypt, a plight that had never been far from Moses' mind, but which had been pushed to the back of his memory. 'I have seen how cruelly my people are being treated,' said the voice. 'I have heard their cries, I know about their suffering.' God was not aloof from human need. He was involved in it. Furthermore, he wanted Moses to be involved in it too. He wanted him to go back to the suffering and the slavery and to do something about it.

This was a bit more than Moses had bargained for! Of course he wanted to help. Of course he was sorry for the slaves. Who wasn't? Of course he wanted to serve God. But wasn't this asking a bit too much of him? It is said that when we want to do something we find time, when we don't want to do it, we find excuses, and this is exactly what Moses did. As he listened to the voice portraying the problem – 'I have seen how the Egyptians are oppressing them' – he agreed with it. But when the voice went on to say, 'I am sending you to rescue them,' he began to protest in a manner which one can either interpret as cowardice or modesty, depending on one's evaluation of Moses' character. Up to that moment he had been a spectator on the sidelines, but now he was being invited to step into the actual arena, and he was not very enthusiastic.

First of all (Ex. 3.11), he told God that he was really a nobody. 'Why pick on me?' he asked. 'How can I go to

41

Pharaoh and tell him to release the slaves? He wouldn't take any notice of me.' That was fair comment and, incidentally, not something that any writer who was an admirer of Moses would have invented. God agreed with Moses. The protest was not met with the bland assurance that he was just the man for the job, but simply with a promise that 'I will be with you and when you bring them out of Egypt you will worship me on this mountain.' That was to be the proof of the promise.

But then Moses thought of something else. He said, 'When I go to the Israelites and tell them that the God of their ancestors has sent me, they will ask me "What is his name?" So what shall I tell them?' That was a much more difficult question than we might think. We might say, with Juliet, 'What's in a name?' but to the ancient Hebrews the name meant the nature and the character of the person, or the god. That was why names were often chosen, or sometimes changed, to suit a character, e.g. when 'Jacob' was changed to 'Israel' (Gen. 32.28). So here Moses was making much more than a protest, he was trying to discover the mystery of the divine nature ... to know the 'name' of God. The answer he got was cryptic and has been the subject of endless speculation ever since. The voice said, 'Tell them I AM has sent you.' In Hebrew, 'I am' is the first person singular of the verb 'h-w-h', meaning, 'to be', or 'to happen'. YH WH is the third person singular of the same verb ... 'he causes to be'. So it seems that Moses was told to tell the Israelites that 'Yahweh', as it is believed the name was pronounced, had sent him. Many years later, when the Hebrew word 'Adonai', or 'Lord' was used instead of Yahweh, the vowels of Adonai and Elohim were combined with the consonants of 'Yhwh', to form the word 'Jehovah'.

There is considerable difference of opinion as to whether the name 'Yahweh' originated with Moses. Some scholars believe that God was known and worshipped as 'Yahweh' from the earliest times, whilst others maintain that the name was introduced only in the time of Moses. It is possible that he learnt of it from the Midianites, through his father-in-law, but the important thing is not how Moses came by that name, but the manner in which he gave it new meaning to the Israelites. There is little doubt that from this time onwards, it meant a God who had heard the cries for help from those under oppression. It stood for a God who intervened on the stage of human history. The I AM was also the one who was 'About to do and be' and 'What he would be'. In Israelite faith, the emphasis became placed on divine activity, not just a promise from a deity with no more than a passive and passing interest. Moses was told that God would reveal himself by his actions, not merely by words: 'Tell them I have decided that I will bring them out of Egypt and will take them to a rich and fertile land.' So Moses' question, 'Who is God?' would be answered by practical proof.

It would be easy to maintain that all this was only in the mind of Moses, as he sat brooding over the fate of the slaves, and that this 'appearance' of God was all imagination. This actually seems to be in the mind of the writer, as he tells of Moses' third objection. 'Suppose the Israelites do not believe me? What shall I say if they say you did not appear to me?' In answer to that, he was told, or taught, to do some pretty dramatic tricks, which seem to fall more into the 'magic' category than the 'miracle'. Indeed, one is inclined to regard what Moses did as the writer's 'proof' for later readers, rather than the answer to Moses' question. He was told to throw his shepherd's staff down on the ground and then it was turned into a snake. He ran away from it, but was told to turn round and grasp it by the tail, and as a result it became a stick again. Then he was told to put his hand inside his cloak and it came out diseased with leprosy, but on putting it back inside and withdrawing it, it was healed. What that was supposed to prove is not clear. Perhaps it was a 'preview' of the kind of Egyptian magical arts we see later on in the story, or perhaps the meaning was mainly symbolic, with the snake representing the problems, or temptations, of the Exodus, which Moses had tended to run away from, but once having faced them and 'grasped them firmly' he found he could master them. If so, the leprous hand would mean the 'strong arm' becoming 'diseased', until the challenge of the burning bush restored it to use again.

Whatever the explanation, Moses was not yet convinced that he was the right man for the job. He made one final plea. 'No Lord, don't send me. I'm a very poor speaker, slow and hesitant.' This, says the story, 'made the Lord angry', though why it should have done so any more than the other objections Moses had made, is not clear. Many years later, Jeremiah was to make the same kind of objection, when God called him to action (Jer. 1.6), and he was told, 'I will be with you to protect you. Do not be afraid.' Moses was told that he would be given a helpmate, in the shape of Aaron his brother, 'for he can speak well'. This introduces Aaron into the story and brings the interview to an end, with Moses having run out of excuses. He went back to Jethro, to tell him that he was returning to Egypt, to begin the rescue operation which has become one of the best-known dramas of all time.

Or has it? The whole Exodus saga is packed with problems, as far as understanding the story is concerned. We have to keep our feet very firmly on the ground and allow for the writers' determination to elaborate on the events, and desire to magnify them into something which almost certainly they were not. We also have to allow for the fact that modern film makers have added to the embroidery by pandering to 'popular' opinion and concept of the stories, rather than sticking to what was probably the plain – and less dramatic – truth. A cartoon in *Punch* some time ago illustrated this fact. It showed a cinema advertising the *Ten Commandments* film and a long queue of people waiting to go in. Across the road, outside a deserted church, a vicar was standing watching them. He was saying to them: 'When you've seen the film, come and read the book.'

If one does read the book, carefully, one realizes that in the matter of most of the plagues, for example, there is a big difference between the film and the book. Almost certainly, the 'miracle' was in the timing of the events, rather than in the events themselves. The river Nile had always played an important part in the life and religion of Egypt. It was regarded and worshipped as a god and giver of life and prosperity, and some of the plagues 'against' it should be seen in this light. When the river was 'turned to blood', in the first plague, it can more easily be understood by pollution than by the picture of Moses standing on the bank, waving his wand and turning the water into blood. A modern writer describes what he saw: 'The red marl brought down the mountains with the melting snows stains the river to a dark colour and in the light of the setting sun it glistens like blood.' After the overflowing of the river, frogs are left high and dry and when they die, flies are not uncommon. More unusual are storms of hail, as in the seventh plague, but they are not unknown, nor are the locusts, or the 'darkness' of the ninth disaster. Sand-storms known as 'Khamsin' can blot out the sun – another Egyptian god – for some time, though one lasting for three days (Ex. 10.21–29) would be unusually severe.

Having said all that, however, to jump to the conclusion that all the plagues belong to the realms of phantasy is as serious an error as to accept them without any reservations whatever. There is a middle way, which is to acknowledge that the writers, looking back on the events from many years later, tended to heighten the miraculous element in order to glorify both the Lord, Moses and the events. In the stories, the plagues are described as 'signs and wonders' and a 'sign' was, to those people, a visible evidence of the presence and purpose of God. To them, the events were 'sign-ificant', not because they were contrary to the rules of Nature, but because they 'proved' God's purpose and presence amongst them. The Exodus was the central point of Israel's faith and such an important part was quite naturally coloured and elaborated by later generations, in the light of that historical experience. The main point they were making was that God was active in history. It was his-story and the stories are an artistic expression of that conviction. The faith was, of course, based on actual events, but over the years those events became more open to imaginative interpretation.

That seems to me to be a reasonable key with which to try and unlock the mysteries of some of these ancient stories, whether of the burning bush, the plagues, the Passover, crossing the Red Sea, and so on. One needs to look carefully at the book rather than at the embroidery. In the incident of the crossing of the sea, for example, a glance at a map will show that Goshen was a long way from the actual Red Sea, even if we regard the Gulf of Suez as an extension of the Red Sea, or even that it extended rather further north than it does today. The confusion was caused when the Old Testament Pentateuch was translated into Greek, in about 250 BC. This became known as the 'Septuagint', or LXX, because it was said to have been done by seventy scholars, but in it the Hebrew words 'Yam Suph' were rendered as 'Red Sea', instead of their actual meaning, which is 'Reed Sea', or 'Papyrus Lake'. Also, since the word 'suph' was usually used to denote reeds growing by fresh water, it seems certain that the crossing of the Reed Sea was in the area around Lake Timsah, or just south of it. This would mean that people on foot would have been able to cross fairly easily, but that iron-wheeled chariots would have sunk in the mud.

All this is not nearly so dramatic, or spectacular as the idea of Moses striking the sea with his rod and the waters all rearing up on end and forming a vast tunnel of water through which the Israelites passed safely and which then collapsed on the pursuing Egyptians, but it is much nearer the truth. The story is told mainly by the J writer, the oldest literary tradition, and it is he who indulges in the kind of anthropomorphism – thinking of God in very human terms – which portrays the Lord as not only fighting for the Israelites but actually clogging the Egyptians' chariot wheels, so that they couldn't move! (Ex. 14.24). Then the E and P writers add their contributions, which tend to add to the drama. According to E, the waters were divided and then returned, by the hand of Moses (Ex. 14.27), whilst P even more vividly, says that the water 'stood up like walls on either side' (Ex.14.22). There is a suggestion here that, in fact, the word 'wall' is used in the sense of a protection in which case the writer meant that the water protected the Israelites from the Egyptian pursuit.

This escape from and defeat of the Egyptians at the Reed Sea represents the final triumph of Moses over Pharaoh, and of Yahweh over the Egyptian gods, but it also raises some very difficult theological concepts as to the nature of a God who 'has triumphed gloriously, throwing horse and rider into the sea' (Ex. 15.21), and generally behaving in a way which prompted one little boy to say that 'God hated all the wicked Egyptians, so he drowned them all to get rid of them'. However, from then on, in the Exodus saga, the Israelites entered upon a new stage of their history. Slavery lay behind them, freedom in front. Yet before they reached their Promised Land they were to learn that slavery is not left behind as easily as all that and freedom is not merely a matter of escaping from a particular people or prison. Wildernesses have a habit of making or breaking people, individually or nationally, by the experiences they bring to bear, mentally, morally or physically. Promised Lands demand a discipline and often a great deal of sacrifice and suffering too, before they can be reached and entered into.

It is easy to be sceptical about Moses' experience at the 'burning bush', perhaps because it cannot be cramped into the precise limits of language. It is much easier to try and reduce it all to the more readable and rational, rather than to the apparently reasonable. But it is also an experience with which the reader can 'identify', with a little imagination. It wasn't just something that happened to a solitary shepherd in the Sinai a very long time ago. It happens to most people at sometime or another, in something they may read, or a picture they may ponder, or a remark they may remember. Such things tend to stay in the mind and they demand a response to the challenge. It is often easier to make excuses than to respond, but the need to act as 'rescuers' will always remain. When we speak of 'slavery' today, we tend to think of it as being abolished, but in fact there are countless millions of people all over the world who could still be said to be slaves, some still physically, others morally, socially and politically. Many more are subject to circumstances, systems and living conditions that make their lives a misery. Some forms of slavery are obvious and well-publicized, from political oppression and tyranny which tolerates no real freedom, to the addiction and dependence on all kinds of drugs that rob the body and mind of rationality and reduces them to a continual quest for escapism and often to crime in order to finance their habit. To be a slave to greed and selfishness brings its own form of solitary confinement, and to be in the grip of moral laxity may seem sophisticated and even look upon as a so-called 'freedom', but in reality it is a prison from which other people are regarded as playthings. Some habits, we are told, die hard, but those that bring degradation also carry their own death sentence with them. We cannot help being human beings, but we can help what kind of human beings we become.

The challenge to fight such slavery is far from over and the need to see certain conditions as slavery and not unavoidable evils is great. The voice came to Moses not only from a bush but from a burning historical situation which was suddenly set alight by his reflection upon it. The voice is never stilled: it is the response that is often suspect. Elizabeth Barrett Browning summed it up very aptly in *Aurora Leigh*:

> Earth's crammed with heaven,
> And every common bush afire with God;
> But only he who sees, takes off his shoes,
> The rest sit round it and pluck blackberries.

4

Joshua and the Walls of Jericho

> Joshua fought the battle of Jericho
> an' de walls came tumblin' down.

To many people, those words may be suitable for an old spiritual song, but they are sceptical and suspicious as to whether the story has any foundation in fact. Furthermore, should the sceptic take the trouble to look at the book of Joshua as a whole, then their credulity may well be strained even futher, with stories of the river Jordan dramatically drying up, the walls of Jericho fortuitously falling down, the sun 'standing still' and the Lord 'throwing down great hail-stones upon the Amorities', all just when Joshua and his men urgently needed a bit of outside help. It may all sound exciting stuff, but to the sombre mind and scrutiny it may well seem more suited to some kind of 'special effects' spectacular than to a serious study of the scriptures!

The first step, therefore, towards any understanding of the saga, is to try and sketch in some kind of background to the stories and to attempt to put the particular and often peculiar events into some kind of perspective and context. One uses the word 'attempt' advisedly, because such efforts are rather like trying to make up a jig-saw which has many of the pieces missing. At first glance, it would appear that we ought to know quite a lot about Joshua and his achievements, but in fact it seems that accurate information is hard to come by. What details that are available seem to be open to so many interpretations and divergent opinions that the picture which emerges is confused rather than clear-cut. Therefore we often have to be content with broad conclusions instead of concise details.

The book of Joshua is described as being 'The story of the Israelite invasion of Canaan under the leadership of Joshua, the successor of Moses', but before the book begins we have already met the main character several times in the Exodus stories and each time he is seen as Moses' 'right-hand' man. When the Israelites were attacked by the Amelekites, for example, during the journey through the desert (Ex. 17.8), Joshua was told to 'pick out some men to go and fight the enemy', which he did and 'totally defeated' them. Later on he was with Moses up on Mount Sinai, as his 'minister', and was the first to recognize that there was something wrong down in the Israelite camp (Ex. 32.17). Then he was one of the twelve spies sent by Moses up into Canaan from the Negeb in the south, to find out what the land was really like (Numb. 13) and on the return, he and Caleb were the only ones who had urged the people to 'go up and possess the land, for we are well able to conquer it,' but the other spies spread such scare stories about all the supposed dangers and difficulties that the people all turned tail and went back into the wilderness.

There can be little doubt, therefore, that Moses regarded Joshua as his staunchest supporter and it was no surprise when he was chosen as Moses' successor when Moses died. He is described as 'full of the spirit of wisdom, for Moses had laid his hands upon him' (Deut. 34.9), and the people were therefore prepared to accept his leadership and his ability to wear the mantle of Moses. His name probably came from the word 'Yehoshuah', which meant 'Jehovah is Salvation', although in Numb. 13.16 he is simply referred to as 'Hoshea', which meant 'salvation'. The name 'Jehoshua' developed into 'Jeshua' and the Greek form of the name became 'Jesus'. So his 'credentials' were sound and with the Israelites poised on the threshold of their so-called 'Promised Land', even though their charismatic leader Moses was no longer at their head, they were prepared to let Joshua take them into the land which they believed was 'flowing with milk and honey', a very ancient expression for a place of fertility and favourable climate.

The name 'Canaan' may have been derived from the Hurrian word 'Kinahu', which meant 'purple' and referred to a precious purple dye extracted from shellfish along the eastern coast of the Mediterranean Sea. It was not considered to be a very large land, at least not in the biblical sense, but it is now clear that it embraced a much larger area. Geographically, it was a land of remarkable diversity and changes in climate, ranging from the cold of the high hills and plateaus down to the tropical heat of the Jordan valley and the wilderness around the Dead Sea. To the Israelites, however, accustomed so long to the barrenness and monotony of the wilderness, it was a place of tremendous potential and possibilities, and a land which would surely match the 'milk and honey' image if only the promise of possession could be fulfilled.

This idea of Canaan being 'promised', however, proved to be the problem! The Israelites may have regarded it as a kind of homecoming to a land their forefathers had left some 400 years before, but since then it had been occupied by tribes collectively known as 'Canaanites' who regarded it very much as their own land and were certainly not going to give it up to a lot of wandering nomads without a struggle, however much the invaders may have imagined that they had some kind of divine right to take it over.

Yet in one sense Canaan was ripe for invasion, as other people apart from the Israelites had discovered. Outwardly the country seemed strong. The Canaanite culture was advanced. Craftsmen produced beautiful works of art from precious metals and pottery, scribes could write letters on clay tablets in cuneiform script, as excavations of the great library at Ugarit on the north Syrian coast have shown, and engineers and architects could build tunnels for water and temples for worship. It was a sophisticated civilization and seemed superior to the Israelites in so many ways that it was perhaps little wonder that the original spies sent in by Moses reported that 'the people who live there are rich and powerful and their cities are large and well-fortified'. Such then, were some of the people, at least, whom the Israelites were to try and dispossess of their land and often of their lives too.

The Canaanites, however, did have a weakness which was to contribute to their downfall, or at least to their discomfiture. They lacked cohesion. The many tribes, including Amalekites, Hittites, Jebusites and Amorites, seemed to have few unifying influences and politically and ethnically it was not a very homogeneous area. Strictly speaking, it was not a 'country' but a collection of 'city states', each ruled over by its own kind and all seeking to exert their independence rather than interdependence. Quarrels between these 'kingdoms' was commonplace and they often lacked the unity and organization that would have given them better protection against attacks. So Joshua's task, though difficult, was not impossible, which is why the book begins with the call to the people to be 'of good courage' and to set their hearts on success.

According to the compiler of the book of Joshua, that success was swift and spectacular. The reader is told how the whole land was overrun in three rapid campaigns, the first being invasion across the Jordan from the east, followed by a victorious strike into the southern hill-country and finally a sweep up into the northern territory around the area later known as Galilee, where a decisive victory at Hazor sealed the successes and made the conquest of Canaan complete. All opposition was overcome and the 'whole land' was 'given to them' because 'the Lord of Hosts fought for Israel'. The completeness of the conquest is indicated in the summary in ch. 11 and the rest of the books, chs 13–20, tells how the land was divided up between the twelve tribes who had taken part. Then the whole campaign was nicely rounded off with Joshua's farewell addresses and warnings in chs 23 and 24.

This view, however, is now seen by most scholars to be much too simple and too 'compressed', and they say that the true picture is probably more complex. They point out that some of the cities said to have been destroyed by Joshua were, in fact, almost certainly sacked long before he got there and that some of the compilers of the stories may well be guilty of 'manipulating' the material a little in order to enhance the events and to further their particular point of view. Such literary 'licence' is not unknown in other parts of the Bible. Scholars also tell us that as far as the literary sources of the book are concerned, since it has a close relationship with the Pentateuch the same traces of J, E, D and P are to be found in Joshua just as they are evident in the first five books of the Bible. They disagree on just how strong is the influence of each source, saying that the book presents as complex a literary problem as any book in the Bible, but suggest that J and E and D are responsible for much of the first twelve chapters, with the D, or Deuteronomic, influence very strong. In which case, the D writer is remembering the promise made to the Patriarchs way back in the book of Genesis, that 'The whole land of Canaan will belong to your descendants for ever' (Gen. 17.8), and is showing how that promise was fulfilled in Joshua's campaigns. But as a result of his religious and theological enthusiasm, he makes the whole thing seem more simple and successful than it really was and even ignores, or sometimes plays down, other elements in the stories which do not fit in with his particular purpose.

It seems, therefore, that the general view is that the book of Joshua is a mixture of material from various sources which reached its present form after a long process of development and deliberation, not to say 'editing' by various interested parties. Can we then appeal to archaeology to provide some answers to the problems? Surely such a period of activities would have provided plenty of evidence, if not actual proof of particular events? The answer seems to be that although a great deal of work has been done and exciting excavations carried out, much of the evidence would appear to be conflicting rather than conclusive. There seems to be considerable argument amongst scholars not only as to how or when the conquest took place, but whether in fact it happened at all in the way the Bible writers present it. Also, apart from an inscription by an Egyptian king Merenpthah, on a stone slab, or 'stele', found at Thebes, which makes it clear that 'Israel' suffered some kind of set-back in Western Palestine at that time, there is very little written evidence for the conquest apart from the Bible record. All this must make the serious student look more carefully at the picture of the invasion as portrayed in the pages of Joshua.

If we do that, we may well begin to wonder what is the book's historical significance and religious message, for the writer's purpose is not to give a colourless 'communiqué', or to write a merely rhetorical report. It is to relate to later Israelite readers the dramatic story of the victorious entry into the Promised Land under the leadership of Joshua. To the writer it was a holy war and a fulfilment of prophecy and promise. He sees his work as the climax and sequel to something which had begun many years before. The 'pattern' had been outlined in Genesis, furthered in the Exodus, when the Israelites had been freed from slavery in Goshen and set on the journey to Canaan, and now had come to a conclusion in Joshua. For such a sequel, he may well have argued, surely a bit of 'embroidery' was not out of place and the 'telescoping' of certain events which may not have happened all at the same time, but could be concentrated in order to popularize a public hero, was permissible. Surely such an exercise as the entry into the Promised Land was worthy of an artist who could be allowed a little licence as long as he painted the picture in bold colours, especially when he was at work several hundred years after the events? After all, some of the Exodus stories had been embellished in order to enhance those events, so why not do the same for Joshua?

Having said that, however, the stories are not to be dismissed as the invention of a later age. They are rooted in history, but in the belief that history is 'his story' and the story of God's dealing with humanity. The fundamental conviction of the editor who has given us Joshua in its present form was that God's mighty acts were performed by human agencies as well as by the forces of Nature. The writer was not worried that readers thousands of years hence might find some of the stories too good to be true. Looking back on the events, he saw the miracles as evidence that God was at work and using every instrument to further his intentions. It was history with a purpose and written with a religious bias, but a drama in which God's hand could be seen in every act.

So the book opens with a clarion call to the people 'to be of good courage and determined, for the Lord your God is with you wherever you go'. No doubt Joshua had in mind the time when he and Caleb had pleaded with the people to go on into Canaan, but lack of courage had meant that many of them died in the wilderness. But now they were back. So Joshua employed the same tactics that Moses had taught him. He told the people that they would be crossing the Jordon, 'to occupy the land the Lord your God is giving you', then, to find out what actually lay ahead, he sent two spies across the river to sound out the city of Jericho, which was the first town that would have to be taken if this invasion from the east was to get a foothold. The way the spies were sheltered and protected by the prostitute Rahab (ch. 2) showed that the spies were only partly successful, but at least they had proved that the place was not impregnable. It may also indicate why Rahab got a 'mention' in Matthew's 'family tree' of Jesus (Matt. 1.5), because of her acknowledgment that 'the Lord your God is God in heaven above and on earth below'. She also obviously believed that the fall of the city was inevitable, for she shrewdly made a bargain with the spies that in return for her keeping them from capture, she and her family would be spared when the city was sacked.

The men reported back to Joshua and so the scene was set for what was obviously going to be seen as a holy war. The people were told to 'sanctify', or 'purify' themselves, which probably meant some kind of ceremonial washing for, they were told, 'tomorrow the Lord will work great wonders among you'. Then the priests, carrying the Ark of the Covenant, or 'Covenant Box', as one translation has it, went down to the river bank, with the people following a respectful distance behind, and when the priests set foot in the Jordan the water 'was brought to a standstill' and 'piled up in a heap' further upstream, making it possible to cross despite the fact that the river was in full spate at that time of the year. The people passed over safely whilst the priests stood in the river and watched. Possibly the passage was helped a little by the twelve big stones that were set up on the river bed, to represent each tribe taking part, and certainly the fact that 'the people passed over in haste' seems to indicate that some at least were not quite certain how long the dam would last! Then, as soon as they were all over, including 'forty thousand fighting men', the river resumed its normal course and 'overflowed its banks as before'.

All this was, of course, very reminiscent of the crossing of the Reed Sea in the time of Moses and no doubt the writer is pointing to the parallel of the Lord being with Joshua 'just as he had been with Moses'. But without wishing to minimize the writer's conviction of divine intervention, it must be pointed out that possibly the miracle was something to do with the timing of what is, in that area, a not uncommon phenomenon, namely that earthquake tremors sometimes cause sections of the high clay buffs to collapse and create a diversion of the waters for a time. This has happened several times in recorded history, the last occasion being in 1927, when the river was twenty-one hours before it returned to 'normal', but the writer of Joshua had no doubt as to the cause or the consequence. He is concerned with the theological significance, not possible geographical explanations. It *happened* and it was opportune, therefore it was the hand of God and it would mean that 'all people on earth will stand in awe of the Lord for ever' (4.24).

Once across, Joshua encamped and considered his next move. The writer says that all the Amorite and Canaanite Kings had heard how the Lord 'had dried up the waters' and 'their courage had melted away', but it still seemed prudent to proceed with caution. A bridgehead had been established, but what now? First, a reminder of religious obligations. Two long-neglected rites were restored: the custom of circumcision was performed again and the Passover, which apparently had

56

not been kept since the escape from Goshen, was renewed. Then, like Moses at the Burning Bush, Joshua had a vision, or 'theophany', when an angel appeared to him, sword in hand. The heavenly messenger, having described himself as 'Commander of the army of the Lord', didn't deliver much of a dialogue and when Joshua asked, 'What does the Lord require of me?' he was told, again like Moses, to 'take off your shoes for the place where you stand is holy ground', which all consolidates the concept of a holy war.

The scene, then, was set for the actual assault on Jericho. The story is told with vivid detail (ch. 6), with the writer revelling in the religious significance and symbolism of it all. The town was said to have been 'shut up, bolted and barred' against the invader, with the inhabitants apparently having a premonition of disaster and defeat at the hands of an enemy on whose side God seemed to be firmly fighting. Yet they must have been puzzled by the appearance of seven priests, armed only with trumpets, followed by a rear-guard carrying the sacred box, who all proceeded to march round the walls in complete silence. They did this once a day for the first six days, then seven times on the seventh day. The number seven was a sacred one, not only for the Israelites but also to other Eastern peoples, especially the Babylonians, so perhaps the significance of this number on this occasion was psychological as well as religious. For the inhabitants of Jericho, already frightened, to see groups of seven men walking round the walls in silence for six days and then the silence suddenly being shattered by the sounding of trumpets and tremendous shouting on the seventh day, must have been unnerving and unnatural.

The shouting was the last straw, as far as the structure of the walls was concerned, for the story simply says that they 'fell down flat'. The reader, however, may well want to ask what evidence there is from archaeology to support such a story. Surely, one suspects, such a spectacular happening should come within the scope of scholars to prove or disprove whether in *c.* 1250 BC, which is the date most prefer for the conquest, it happened or not. The question sounds simple, but the answers are complex. It is certainly true that Jericho has been a favourite target for archaeologists ever since the Palestine Exploration Fund was founded in 1865 to conduct biblical excavations. This is hardly surprising, since Jericho is not only the lowest inhabited place in the world, being 820 feet below sea level and about five miles north of the Dead Sea, but it is also the oldest walled town in the world we yet know of, with radio-carbon dating of some of the fortifications giving a date of around 10,000 BC. There have been numerous expeditions and some exciting and important discoveries, but the conclusions seem to be sometimes conflicting. An operation in the 1930s found evidence that certain sections of the walls had indeed collapsed and parts had been burnt. This did not mean that the walls had all fallen down like a pack of cards or that the whole of the city had been burnt, but certainly there had been violent destruction and foodstuffs found in the ruins indicated that it had happened at the time of harvest, which ties up with the writer's contention that this was the time when it happened (4.15). The stumbling-block, however, seemed to be that this destruction was dated by the archaeologists at about 1400 BC, which is much earlier than the generally accepted date of the conquest.

Then an expedition in the 1950s concluded that Jericho had been a great city until it was destroyed even earlier than 1400 BC and that after that it was only spasmodically occupied by settlers, which would have meant that Joshua's men found a city which was no longer prosperous or powerful, probably with gaps left in the walls from previous attacks and therefore the original over-running of the town could not be credited to Joshua. In fact, Dame Kathleen Kenyon, who led the 1950s expedition, went as far as to say that Jericho may have been nothing more than a ruin when Joshua arrived, if the date of the conquest is correct. Other archaeologists dispute this conclusion.

The same can be said of the next town Joshua had to take, a place called Ai, although here the evidence seems to be more conclusive. The word 'Ai' in Hebrew meant 'ruin' and the site has been extensively excavated. It would seem clear that there was a thriving city there *c*. 3000 BC, but that it was violently destroyed *c*. 2400 BC and abandoned, with no further significant occupation of the place being made until the start of the Iron Age, *c*. 1200 BC. This indicates that Ai really was a ruin when Joshua arrived and had been in that state for many years. So possibly the story may have been told to explain how the place got its name, or perhaps the ruin was used by various tribes for shelter and refuge in times of trouble, and Joshua's men merely 'flushed out' some squatters who were doing just that. Certainly it may explain why Joshua's spies, sent in to reconnoitre, found little evidence of occupation on their first visit (7.3).

In the case of Hazor, which Joshua is said to have destroyed in his northern campaign, the evidence seems to bear out the Bible story better. The archaeologists tell us that at one time it was a city of some 30–40,000 people, but it suffered dramatic destruction *c*. 1225 BC and was never rebuilt until the time of Solomon. This fits in well with both the date of the conquest and the Biblical description of its destruction (11.10–13), but that doesn't prevent some scholars being sceptical and pointing out that the city could well have been burnt by someone else, Egyptians or Babylonians for example, since the thirteenth century BC was a very turbulent time in Canaan and destruction of towns was commonplace. Therefore, to prove that a place was razed by any particular person or peoples is very difficult.

So it seems that we have several schools of thought on the events described in Joshua. Some support the quick campaign idea and accept the stories as they stand. Others prefer to think that the conquest was not achieved in one fell swoop, but by different incursions by different groups at various times, and these separate events were later combined by the Bible writers to form one story and one conquest under one leader. Joshua, they say, did conduct a campaign, but the whole conquest was spread over a much longer period. Another theory is that the whole thing was more of a gradual infiltration, with the Israelites content to collaborate with the occupying tribes and eventually settling down to live amongst them. Still another idea is that the Israelite occupation was in fact aided and abetted by some kind of revolt by elements in Canaan who were dissatisfied by the conditions under which they lived and welcomed an opportunity to overthrow the system – a kind of social and religious revolution which Joshua's men were able to use to advantage. My own view is that there is really no need to take every detail of the Joshua stories as literal truth, since there are indications both in the book itself and in the first chapter of Judges that the conquest was not as quick and complete as the editors would have us believe.

The rational and impartial reader may well be able to accept all this. There is little doubt that the Israelites did settle in Canaan sometime during the thirteenth century BC and since every conquest and war in history has its share of stories which can be looked upon as legendary, and achievements and attributes assigned to leaders which it is very doubtful whether they deserved, a bit of bias by the Bible writers can be understood. But what many a modern reader finds difficult to understand and accept is what happened to the inhabitants of various cities when Joshua attacked them, whether the numbers are exaggerated or not. We read that in the case of Jericho, Ai and Hazor, Joshua gave his men specific instructions as to what they had to do. They were to go in when the town fell and put every single living thing to the sword, 'young and old, men and women, cattle, sheep and asses'. No one was to be spared, except at Jericho where Rahab and her family were left alive.

The word used for this wholesale slaughter was 'herem' and it denoted something that was 'set apart' from common use and 'devoted' to the deity. It was not just a sacrifice, it was absolute alienation from common consideration and was often looked upon as a kind of 'thanksgiving' to the god who had given an army victory. Jericho, Ai and Hazor are specially singled out for this 'ban', or 'curse', and this meant the complete destruction of all life and the 'cleansing' of the cities by fire. All precious possessions had to be 'dedicated' to holy use by putting them 'in the treasury of the Lord'. These things were sacred, so they must not be stolen but set apart for religious purposes. Underlying this practice was probably the belief that whatever may 'contaminate' the life and religion of a people must be destroyed but what was 'pure', like gold for example, could be set aside for sacred use. The writer makes no bones about it – in the case of Jericho, 'the city and everything in it must be totally destroyed as an offering to the Lord', at Ai 'the number who were killed was twelve thousand', and at Hazor, 'they killed every living thing in it and spared nothing that drew breath'.

So we have the strange phenomenon of regarding the entire population of a city as candidates for wholesale slaughter, but their possessions as something to be spared and preserved. In fact, the first attempt to capture Ai met with failure because, so it was said, someone had broken the rules at Jericho about precious possessions and a man named Achan was condemned as the culprit. He was singled out for stoning, along with all his family and animals, because he had 'coveted' some silks and silver and gold, and had hidden them beneath his tent. When the stoning had been carried out, everyone felt relieved that 'the Lord's anger had been abated' and they were then free to get on with the job. One wonders how many other looters there had been, who were just as guilty as Achan but who joined in the stoning of the 'scapegoat' in the hope that it would divert attention away from them. 'Achanism' may not be a word in the dictionary, but it is certainly a trait in human nature, as we have seen in so many national and political scandals over the years.

To many a modern mind, even in days when barbarism and bloodshed have become so blatant and commonplace, such acts of brutality as described in the book of Joshua are repugnant and repulsive, and an inexcusable violation of human dignities and decencies. The reader recoils at the very idea that such things were done at the command, so it was claimed, of God. How could the writers apparently condone the kind of annihilation and massacre usually associated with atrocities and cruelties of the worst possible kind and how could they justify the slaughter of innocent people whose only crime was that they happened to have lived in places that lay in the path of an invader who wanted to oust them from their homes and take possession of their land?

The essential thing to remember is that the whole campaign was seen as a holy war and in such circumstances terrible things are done in the name of religion. Both ancient and modern history can provide plenty of examples of that. In the catalogue of the causes of war, religion must take its place alongside such things as politics and lust for power. Whatever else we may know or not know about Joshua, he represents the concept of what we may call the war-god, and in a sense it was understandable because no other concept could have answered for the task he undertook. Whatever interpretation of the conquest one may accept, there was fighting to be done and it could only be carried out by a fanaticism which was best generated by the idea of a holy war. It roused what could be called the 'battle-fury' and Joshua exploited this to the full. The Lord was seen as fighting exclusively on the side of the Israelites and therefore what they did was 'right', whilst the other side, since they were 'enemies' of the Lord and pagans, must be in the wrong. It was, to them, quite clear-cut and any arguments about whether the actions were right or wrong would have been a waste of time. It is a principle which is often propagated, even by those who profess to have no prejudice. 'Let me put it like this,' said a member of a particular religious sect to me recently. 'You people are floundering in the water. We are the only ones on the boat.'

In warfare, a soldier doesn't often exercise the privilege of private judgment. He tends to obey orders and can then claim that he personally was not answerable for the consequences. He can come to regard human life as expendable and may well adopt the attitude of 'It's either them or me.' But in a 'holy' war a person can take life not for revenge, or even hatred. He or she can do so for an ideal, a conviction that they have some kind of divine right to do it because of race, religion or ideology. When people become convinced that what they are doing, however repulsive, is completely in accordance with the will of their God, or at the direct command of a religious leader, they can do the most dreadful things without compassion or compunction, and can 'justify' almost any act of aggression. Add to that, in some cases, a promise that to lay down one's life fighting the 'heathen' means a 'front row' in paradise, and there can be a most deadly combination of cruelty and callous disregard for the value of human life. During the last war, Japanese bomber pilots willingly went on suicide missions with this Shinto assurance, and Mr Amir Taheri, an Iranian editor and author, now living in Paris, writing on the very rapid spread of Islam in the world, says that in many cases, 'The image of Islam is becoming increasingly associated with violence, terrorism and repression,' and this is due, he says, in no small measure to the activities of extreme Muslim fundamentalists. Indeed, he cites one of the dictums of the late Ayatollah Khomeini, to his army in Iran, as being 'To kill and to get killed is the supreme duty of every true Muslim.'

In Joshua's case, the destruction and killing was cold and calculated. In their 'clinical' operations, they regarded themselves as God's 'instruments' to carry out his purpose and plan, which to them was the taking over of the land and the destruction of everything that might 'contaminate' Israelite life and religion. It was not a matter of taking vengeance, or of committing atrocities in the sense that occupying armies are given the 'spoils of war', which often means a licence to do whatever they like to conquered peoples and their possessions, as the world has seen so often. It was rather seen as a divine duty which they were to perform as efficiently as possible, with no half-measures.

We must also bear in mind the moral and religious climate which pervaded in Israel at the time when the book of Joshua was compiled, which according to many scholars was sometime during the eighth century BC, and which the writers would have very much in mind. It was a time when religious compromise with all kind of pagan practices was commonplace and when prophets like Amos and Hosea highlighted

63

the social and moral morass into which the nation had fallen, and the writers of 'Joshua' looked back to the conquest and from it drew lessons from their own day and age. They felt that the people should be reminded that any compromise with evil was contaminating and that loyalty to the Lord was vital if the nation was to survive. They viewed anything which derrogated their religious resolve as disastrous, and reckoned that whatever weakened true worship of Jahweh should be rooted out.

We can therefore condemn the crudeness of Joshua's campaign and criticize those who condoned the 'war-god' concept, but we may well be left with a feeling that the book has a message for our modern day. Even allowing for possible exaggerations, doubts and difficulties, it shows a leadership and resolve to overcome opposition despite what must have seemed at the time almost impossible odds and a fierce determination to fight whatever they believed would betray their beliefs. The writers saw the very life of Israel being threatened and undermined by subversive elements in their own day and were convinced that the same principles should still apply. This is surely worth remembering today, when the Christian church is under constant fire for not maintaining moral standards, for failing its founder and its followers, and for being afraid to fight the enemies who are bringing this nation to a moral decline in our society as dramatic as any in history. It is obvious to all but the very ostrich-like that we face problems no slick solutions can solve. A leading article in an influential newspaper recently pointed out that 'Whilst some things in our society are still "sacred", the things it is still safe to decry are decency and dignity.'

Before Joshua died, he warned the people of the dangers which lay ahead in Canaan. In his 'farewell address' (ch. 24), he challenged them to 'Choose this day whom you will serve' and they promised to 'serve the Lord'. But when they entered the 'new age' of the Promised Land, many Israelites were caught up in the Canaanite ways of worship, which placed considerable emphasis on the erotic in the association with the fertility gods and godesses, and the gods they then chose to serve were those which seemed to be fashionable and sophisticated. The book of Joshua ends with the statement that 'Israel served the Lord during the lifetime of Joshua and of the elders who outlived him, who knew what the Lord had done for Israel,' but then the book of Judges shows that on many occasions the 'walls' which defended their faith fell down even more easily than those at Jericho had done!

5

Jonah and the Big Fish

This is the story which not only gives many people the excuse for ridicule, but which also lends itself to such puns as 'the story which is hard to swallow', and 'Jonah having a whale of a time'. The important thing, however, is not what the readers are expected to believe but to which readers we refer. For it is the modern reader who tends to create the difficulties and complications which confuse the issues and which rob the story of its real meaning. The original readers would have had no such problems in seeing the point of the parable, for they would have recognized the story for exactly what it was intended to be – a parable. That is the first step towards any serious study of this little book! To take as literal truth what is so obviously intended as a moral tale is not only insulting to the original writer's intentions, but is also to lack the sense of humour which so often can rescue religion from the realm of the ridiculous.

The book of Jonah is a superb work of art, painted by a prophet who would surely turn in his grave at the thought of his work being 'touched up' by those who regard themselves as 'restorers', but who actually add to the layers which obscure the original. In that sense, and for that reason, the book of Jonah has probably been more unfortunate in the treatment it has received than any other book in the Bible. Unlike the

Jonah and the Big Fish

book of Esther, for example, or the Song of Solomon, which
seem to be much more erotic than religious, but which have
been credited with religious meanings which in my view they
never deserved and probably never intended, Jonah has so
often been denied the depths of insight and examination that
the writer so undoubtedly deserves and displays. Instead of
being a stepping-stone to greater understanding of vital
issues, it has become for many people a stumbling-block to
taking the Bible seriously. It tends to bear out the contention
that there are three types of attitudes towards some of these
stories; there are people who take them strictly literally,
people who regard them as rubbish, and people who really
read them.

Those who tend to take this story literally point to the fact
that in the first verse of the book, the chief character is
referred to as 'Jonah, son of Amittai' and therefore, they
conclude, the story must be historical. They also point out
that Jesus, in Mat. 12.39–41, spoke of 'Jonah being in the
belly of the whale for three days', so who are we to argue?
Granted, there is a 'Jonah, son of Amittai' mentioned in
II Kings 14.25, who came from a place called Gath-hepher
and must have lived about 780 BC, since he was something to
do with Jeroboam II, who was King of Israel at that time.
Therefore the assumption is that since Jonah is mentioned in
Israelite history, the book must have a historical foundation.
Such reasoning is rather risky and can lead to false conclu-
sions. For example, could we, by that same token, assume that
since Thomas Becket was part of English history, Eliot's
Murder in the Cathedral must be taken as literal truth?

The use of a historical figure was surely to remind the
readers that Jonah was a commissioned prophet, like all
the other great prophets of the past. But the difference is that
although the book is found in the section of the Bible called
the Prophets, it differs from the other books of the prophets
because it gives no idea of the writer's identity. Also, although
it gives a great deal of information about what the prophet
did, it tells us very little of what he said. The point was that
Jonah was going to be a man sent by God and that God would

work through him, just as he had worked and spoken through all the other prophets. Having established that, in the first verse, the writer's purpose has been served and no other mention of Jeroboam's adviser is made in the book. No doubt, some tradition associated with the historical prophet, possibly that he was a person who was very sure of himself, made him a very appropriate character around which to build the parable. Perhaps the writer was being rather ironic in making use of the prophet's name, in order to give more point to his parable. After all, for such a man to change his ways and see someone else's point of view would have been a real 'coup', as far as conversion was concerned!

To say that Jesus' reference to Jonah proves that the story was factual is rather like saying that Jesus must have known the Prodigal Son or the Good Samaritan personally. Jesus certainly would recognize a good parable when he saw one, and here he was referring to a well-known story which all his hearers would know, but that is no reason for believing that either he or they would take it literally. He was using the parable to drive home a particular point which he was trying to make, which was about his own experience of rejection, death and resurrection. Even a casual reading of the Gospels shows that Jesus, especially in John's Gospel, uses symbolic language on occasions to describe an important truth and is sometimes taken literally by his listeners. But that is their fault, not his. A modern preacher would be somewhat surprised if after referring to *The Pilgrim's Progress* in a sermon, he was afterwards accused of taking Bunyan's allegory as actual fact!

In any case, Jesus is said to have referred to the three days in which 'Jonah spent in the whale's belly', but the word 'whale' is never mentioned in the book of Jonah at all. The actual translation is 'a great fish' and only three verses of the forty-eight verses in the book make any mention of the monster at all. Yet those three verses have been blown up out of all proportion to their importance and most people know the story only because of them. They read – or far more likely just hear – of a man who was swallowed by a 'whale' and then regurgitated some time later apparently none the worse for his time spent 'inside', and they become even more convinced that the Bible is filled with fairy tales.

This position is made even stronger, though unwittingly, by those who maintain that such monsters have been found, who have swallowed a man who has managed to survive. Like the story of a certain Mr James, a whale hunter, who, in 1891, was said to have been swallowed by a whale and then taken alive out of its stomach when the creature was killed. I am not saying that it was impossible, but I am saying that it is not remotely what the story of Jonah is about. To imagine that it is, is to suffer from a shortsightedness which prevents a focus on the book's real philosophy. Although found amongst the 'minor' prophets, because of its length, the little book is of major importance, and to those who can take their eyes off the 'whale' and concentrate instead on the wisdom, it has proved to be a 'burning bush' before which they have felt like taking off their shoes, because they sensed it was holy ground.

What, then, is the book's real value and importance? As far as we can tell, it was probably written shortly after the return of the Jews from the Exile in Babylon (586–539 BC), though some scholars put it as late as some time between 400–350 BC. They point to the narrowness of Jonah's outlook and say it reflects the kind of exclusiveness envisaged by Ezra in c. 440 BC. Certainly, in 3.3 it seems that Nineveh, the capital city of Assyria, is spoken of in the past tense and the description of it as a city 'taking three days to cross' indicates a looking back from a much later date with, as so often happens, the magnifying of events and places accordingly. Even if Jonah was a fast walker it would have meant a journey of about thirty or forty miles and a city of such proportions was unknown in the ancient world. Indeed, a survey of Nineveh, published over a hundred years ago, estimated that even at its widest extent, the city would be less than four miles across. In addition, certain phrases and words used in the book, such as 'the God of heaven' (1.9), are only found in later Hebrew writings. So it seems that a late date is indicated.

The point to bear in mind is that for many Jews the

destruction of Jerusalem in 586 BC had seemed like the end of the world and the subsequent exile in Babylon did little to lessen the intense feelings of bitterness and resentment against those who had descecrated and destroyed their holy city. Indeed, one of the very few pieces of writing to come out of Exile, Ps. 137, shows a desire for revenge probably unequalled in all the Old Testament. Many of those who returned, under the leadership of Nehemiah and Ezra, settled down to the rebuilding of Jerusalem, but many also revived and remembered the feelings of resentment as far as foreigners were concerned. They had forgotten the words of God to Moses (Ex. 13.19), 'I will be gracious to whom I will be gracious and I will have compassion on whom I will have compassion', and also the vision of 'Second' Isaiah, the prophet who had writen during the Exile itself (ch. 55).

What many Jews in that post-exilic period needed was for someone to remind them of their real calling and of the reason for their being brought out of Egypt in the Exodus, which was to have a missionary outlook on the rest of the nations. They had forgotten that 'God is no respecter of persons ... you must love the alien, for you were once aliens in Egypt' (Deut. 10.17). They needed someone with the skill of a spiritual surgeon to correct their moral eyesight, enabling them to see that the narrow nationalism of Nehemiah and Ezra was too much like tunnel vision. The writer of the book of Jonah proved to be that physician and the instrument he used was the one which had been used by the prophets before him, and which was to be used to such effect by Jesus many years later – the parable.

One of the previous prophets who had used the parable as a pointer to moral judgment was Nathan. He had witnessed the sordid spectacle of David's affair with Bathsheba, which resulted in David having Uriah, Bathsheba's husband, killed in battle, in order to remove the embarrasment of him finding out that his wife was going to have David's child, (II Sam. 11). Nathan went to David and told him the parable of the rich man who had plenty of sheep from which to choose one for a gift for a visitor, but instead he stole the only lamb of a poor man. David, thinking that he was being asked to make a moral judgment, exclaimed in indignation, 'Such a man deserves to die!' To which Nathan replied, 'Yes – and you are that man.' It was the clever technique of leading the listener into thinking that the judgment was for someone else, then being brought to realize that the real condemnation should be upon themselves.

So it is with the Jonah parable, and it is the reason why the book ends so abruptly. The point had been made; any further comment was unnecessary and superfluous. The writer had set the scene by portraying a prophet who, when told by God to go and preach to the people of Nineveh, immediately made off in the opposite direction. That was a very clever beginning to the story. It would immediately attract the attention of the readers, because that would seem to them the most sensible and obvious thing for Jonah to do. Who on earth would want to even visit a place like Nineveh, let alone preach to its people? Was it not the capital city of the hated and dreaded Assyrians, who had been responsible for so much suffering? When they had invaded Israel and had finally starved Samaria into surrender in 721 BC, their brutality and atrocities had been too terrible to talk about. Therefore, when the writer chose Nineveh as the prophet's proposed preaching place, he would be on safe ground in thinking that his readers would shudder at the very thought. They would roundly applaud Jonah's refusal to go anywhere near it, even though he had been told to 'denounce the city'.

So it was no surprise to see Jonah sailing off to Tarshish, probably a place in southern Spain and as far away west across the Mediterranean as ships in those days tended to go. The name Jonah probably meant 'dove', but he didn't seem to have much of the spirit of gentleness and peace about him, though from the start he is seen not as a coward but as a man who thought he knew what God wanted him to do but had decided that such demands were asking too much. He also suspected that God was somehow not seeing things his way, so therefore the best policy was one of non-co-operation. After all, a little show of religious independence occasionally did no harm, especially when a grass-roots opinion seemed more practical than the long-term view. Jonah had been called to be a preacher and a prophet, but had turned down the invitation. It wasn't that he thought he could run away from God's presence, but he wanted to get away from God's pressure. He wanted to do his own thing, as far as religion was concerned, and on his own terms. He preferred his own prejudice to God's power and the point which the writer was making was that this attitude was tantamount to turning one's back on God.

As Jonah settled down to his sea trip, he was confident that he had made the right choice. He went down to a corner of the ship and was soon sleeping the sleep of the just, confident that a rather thorny theological problem had been solved. But though Jonah may have thought that was the end of it, God was only just beginning! He sent such a storm upon the boat that it seemed about to break into pieces and the superstitious seamen wondered what they had done to deserve such a disaster. They came to the conclusion that someone on board was bringing them bad luck, so they cast lots to see who it was and the finger of suspicion was soon pointing at the prophet or, as the writer put it, 'The lot fell on Jonah!' The sailors questioned him closely and, as the writer carefully makes clear, behaved towards Jonah in a most considerate manner. These heathen men, whose kind Jonah apparently didn't consider very worthy of God's attention, were so concerned that when Jonah offered to let himself be thrown overboard as a kind of sacrifice to quieten the sea, they did their utmost to reach land and make his sacrifice unnecessary. Only when this proved impossible did they agree to jettison Jonah.

A nice little touch that! A good example of a spiritual psychologist writer with his finger very much on the pulse of human nature. Jonah had despised foreigners from a distance, but at close quarters and as individuals, they seemed much more likeable. He had refused to go and preach to a heathen city, but now he offers to sacrifice his own safety and security to save a few frightened Gentile sailors. The point was that Jonah saw fit to make this kind of gesture on his own account. He could be merciful to the heathen if he chose, as an individual and on a small scale, but he still thought that as a general principle God needed to keep them at arm's length. Jonah's personal atttiude could be one of being merciful, but the 'official' policy should be one of stern judgment. So the writer-physician gently points to the very condition which has to be cured, if the patient is to recover. Jonah was acting with what he saw as noble resolve, but with little evidence of any repentance for his shortcomings. He told the sailors that he was sorry to have caused them so much trouble, but he didn't say anything about being sorry for the citizens of Nineveh. Apparently a few harmless sailors, literally in the same boat as Jonah, were one thing, but a whole nation, whom he had never met, were another.

However, overboard he went and the sea calmed down, which is where the 'whale' came into the story, though the word is never mentioned. Whatever description of the 'monster' is used, the idea is the same. The theme of a monster from the deep, or sometimes from the land, swallowing a person, or persons, was old before Jonah's time. It is found in the folk-stories of many ancient peoples, and its purpose was always the same – to represent some kind of disaster which befell and individual or tribe, from which they were later rescued or recovered. So the writer was using a well-known formula to illustrate the point he was making about the Exile in Babylon and the return from it. Such symbolism seems obvious when we remember that Jeremiah had described the Exile in very much the same way: 'Nebuchadrezzar king of Babylon has devoured me, like a dragon he has swallowed me ... I will punish Bel in Babylon and make him bring up what he has swallowed' (Jer. 51.35,44).

The writer of the Jonah story obviously sees the Exile as a judgment on the Jewish people for failing to recognize that their special calling as a nation was not a guarantee of privilege and prestige, but a responsibility to bear witness to God's goodness and mercy to all men. Jonah personified those who had refused to respond to God's requirements and who had run away from certain responsibilities. The Exile had been a dark and dreadful experience, but they had been delivered from it, just as Jonah had been thrown up on to dry land, and were then required to make God's purpose known to the world, which included Gentiles as well as Jews. But even the Exile had not taught some of them this lesson and they were just as exclusive as their forefathers had been. So the writer used Jonah to highlight the lesson they should have learnt. As biology the 'big fish' is decidedly dubious, but as symbolism it is superb.

From inside the fish Jonah prays, in words which are extracts from various psalms and which again suggest Exile, for 2.4 indicates that he is far removed from the temple where he used to worship, but that 'deliverance belongs to the Lord'. His prayer is heard and answered. He is delivered and then he is told again to go to Nineveh. This time, ch. 3, he agrees to go and in fact begins to relish the prospect of proclaiming 'Jonah's judgment' on all and sundry. He lost no time in informing them that in forty days disaster would fall upon them, but no sooner had the count down started than he had a severe shock and setback. Not only did everyone listen to him, which he had not anticipated, but the whole city, from the king down to the lowest peasant, responded to his preaching by repenting, in sack-cloth and ashes.

This was the kind of success Jonah hadn't expected or bargained for. Instead of being delighted he was very dismayed and instead of being pleased he was most put out. He told God not to be taken in by such a turn-about. It was a trick! Nineveh was doomed – hadn't God told him to 'go and denounce it'? He had kept his part of the bargain, now he expected God to keep his. 'Forty days and Nineveh shall be overthrown' had been his brief and Jonah couldn't remember anything about repentance in those instructions. So what had gone wrong with the arrangements?

Nothing had gone wrong, except that Jonah was jumping to conclusions which had never been considered. He had not only made up his own mind, but he was trying to tell God what to do too. 'Don't listen to them, Lord,' he said, in effect. 'They don't mean it. Their penitence is a put-up job.' But God

74

was listening to them and there was a danger that he would not bring upon them the doom and disaster that Jonah had predicted. This made Jonah so upset that he told God that he would now be better off dead. There was nothing left to live for. So we see another example of the writer's irony, the delicate touch in this wonderful work of art. Jonah had told God (4.2–3) that although he is greatly disappointed and displeased at these developments, it was really what he had been afraid of right from the start: 'I knew you are a gracious and compassionate God, long-suffering and ever constant' (4.2–3). Jonah was not only saying that he thought this might happen, he was actually trying to justify the way in which he had behaved. He was saying that because he had secretly suspected that God might be soft with the sinners, he had adopted his harsh attitude in order to counteract the possibility. This all added up, according to Jonah's reckoning, that he had been right all along.

The trouble was that although he was ready to admit that God was merciful and of great kindness, Jonah didn't want these qualities to be put into practice, because it wouldn't fit into Jonah's diagnosis on how God ought to operate. Therefore, still convinced that he was right and it was God who had got it wrong, the prophet, having expressed the desire to die, retired to a hillside outside the city to await developments. The sun was very hot and Jonah was very bothered, so he built a shelter for some shade, but when a 'gourd', or castor-oil plant, suddenly grew up from nowhere and afforded him further shade, he was very glad of it. But the joy was short-lived because the next morning the plant suddenly perished, leaving Jonah once more exposed to the sun and to the desire to die. He was very upset about the way in which the plant had let him down and he told God that he had every right to be.

Then came the punch-line with which the parable ends. The Lord said to Jonah, 'You are very upset about one plant, which lived and died without any help from you, but don't you think you ought to be far more concerned about the people in Nineveh – a hundred and twenty thousand of them?' The question is not answered, because there is no need. Jonah's perverseness had been exposed to the light and the point had been clearly made. The writer leaves it to the reader's intelligence and conscience to work out what it meant. Jonah had shown a concern that was really mostly self-interest. He had been taught that God was a God of mercy and grace, yet failed to see how the theory could be put into practice. Like the elder son in the parable of the Prodigal Son, he had thought that he knew what his father wanted, but his 'keeping to the rules' had not given him a good relationship with his father or with his brother, nor had it given him an understanding about concern and compassion for the 'sinner'.

Of course, the writer of the Jonah parable is exaggerating in order to prove his point, just as Jesus sometimes did and just as great writers have often done. He is pointing to an extreme example and attitude and we cannot imagine that all the Jews returning from the Exile were as bigoted towards the Gentiles as was Jonah, any more than we can say that all Pharisees and tax-collectors were either as pompous or as pious as the two men portrayed in Jesus' parable on prayer (Luke 18). But equally we must admit that many Jews did share Jonah's prejudice, either openly or secretly, and that the lesson of God loving the 'lost' as well as the 'righteous', was a hard one to learn. There is ample evidence, both from the Gospels and from the Acts of the Apostles, that many Jews had still not accepted the fact that 'God had no favourites', even by the time of Jesus and Paul.

It is not really surprising that today the Jewish people prefer to read the book of Jonah on their day of Atonement, for its theme is not only a promise of reconciliation between God and man, but also a plea for a common humanity. We cannot separate a belief in the brotherhood of man from the fact of the Fatherhood of God. Nor can we escape the reality, however much we may try to evade it, that the mercy of God is for all men. Many people have the curious conception that if one is of a particular race, or colour, or language, or religion, that somehow makes them 'chosen' or 'special', and more important to God than those who may differ in these respects. On the other hand, however, there are those who go to the other extreme and give the impression that God cares more for those of another race or religion than for one's own. They bend over backwards to discredit their own nation or denomination, whilst continually extolling the virtues of every other creed and culture.

Here again, the writer has a word for such unbalanced attitudes. Not only does he point to the importance of tolerance, but also to the danger of pretending that there are no problems as far as differing races and religions are concerned. In his story, there is nothing sentimental about the situation, no whitewashing of wickedness and no discrimination either for or against a particular people. The true position is recognized and acknowledged, because the writer realizes that only by doing that can any real solution be found. So the sins of both Nineveh and Jonah are highlighted – Jew and Gentile. They are both contrasted to the mercy of a God who is not only shown as being at work in human history, but also having to use human agency to do that work. Jonah, as it were, highlights the kind of difficulties God faces when he decides to make certain people his messengers!

The question is sometimes asked, 'What happened to Jonah? Did he ever change and see God's purpose, or did he persist in his efforts to resist it?' The answer, as far as the actual story goes, is that we do not know, since there is no mention of his fate or future, but as far as moral truth goes, which is the point of the parable, the answer is that Jonah never dies so long as his attitudes are still alive. Whenever and wherever there is hatred, injustice, religious restrictive practices, and a belief that God is 'localized' in one particular sect or society, or even church building, then Jonah is still very much alive and active, and still sits outside many a city telling God that the people inside do not deserve his mercy.

Of course, it would be foolish to suggest that everyone in Nineveh was really repentant. It may well have been that in some cases the fear of a day of disaster and reckoning did far more to foster a desire to change their ways than any genuine change of heart. People do sometimes become 'converted' when crisis comes! It could also be said that as soon as the fortieth day had passed and no disaster had descended upon them, many people soon forgot their good intentions and went back to their former ways. But the fact remains that the book of Jonah casts it own condemnation on those who think it has nothing to say to them.

That is why the parable is so perennial and why its truths are always valid. Religion and race are not restrictions, but responsibilities. They are not exclusive, they should be inclusive. Selfish interests should never be as important as people in need and no sect or party should imagine that they can 'corner the market' as far as salvation is concerned. God's love, as Charles Wesley puts it, is 'immense and unconfined', and open to all who will respond to it. If we could see Jonah in this light, we could forget it being a bit of a 'fishy' story and its truth would not be something which, for the want of understanding, was the 'one that got away'.

6

Daniel and the Lions' Den

Just as the Jonah story has been largely associated with a whale, so the story of Daniel and his friends becomes, in the minds of many people at least, almost exclusively linked with a den of lions or a fiery furnace, and often with the same, sad results. If the desire is to dwell on the lions' den or to focus entirely on the fiery furnace, there is a great danger that the rest of the story and its real meaning will be lost, yet in the minds of many people that is about all they very vaguely remember about Daniel. Also, as with the Jonah parable, the book of Daniel has become a happy hunting ground for those who insist on taking every word as literally true and a mine from which they quarry all kinds of strange prophecies for the future. They point out that the book comes under the heading of 'apocalyptic' writing and since that word means 'to reveal', they see in it all kinds of revelations for the future. Of course, hidden meanings are implied, especially in the visions of Daniel, in chapters seven to twelve, because when the book was written to say straight out what was actually meant would have been a risky business, but forecasting the future, in the way some maintain, was not the writer's purpose or intention.

It used to be referred to as a 'sealed' book, but under the scrutiny of modern scholarship and research, it has acquired a reputation far removed from its supposed 'prophecies and predictions' purpose. It falls quite naturally into two sections, chapters one to six telling the stories of Daniel and his friends, and chapters seven to twelve describing Daniel's visions, with some of the book being written in Aramaic rather than in Hebrew, though this is not confined to any particular part. Since the whole book is too long to be dealt with in this short survey, we can conveniently concentrate on the first section, where, it would seem, the writer has used material from several sources to suit his own purpose. But what was his purpose? What lies behind such spectacular stories as men being thrown into circumstances of certain death, only to emerge unscathed, or such strange events as the ghostly writing on the wall at Belshazzar's feast? The stories have since inspired great works of art and music, but what was the original writer trying to tell us? The answers must lie in a closer look at the background to the book and the circumstances in which it was written.

When Alexander the Great died in Babylon, in 323 BC, he was only thirty-two years of age and there are various theories as to how he came to die so young. Some say that he died of a disease, probably malaria, whilst others maintain that he was a hopeless alcoholic and drank himself to death, or even took his own life, but the fact remains that before he died he had succeeded in conquering most of the ancient world. One legend has it that he stood on the banks of the Indus river 'weeping that he had no more worlds to conquer', but no doubt there were one or two places he had missed! Certainly he was an amazing young man. Taught by the great Greek philosopher and thinker, Aristotle, and strongly influenced by Homer's *Iliad*, he had long dreamed of a world bound together, or dominated, depending on how one regards such an ambition, by the Greek way of life, culture and language. Such a policy became known as 'Hellenism', from the world 'Hellas', the ancient name for Greece.

Alexander did not live to see what he saw as a divine mission fully accomplished, but there is little doubt that his dream was the driving force which spurred him on to such remarkable military success. At its best, Hellenism contained many lofty intellectual, artistic and aesthetic ideals and many a city in the ancient world became enriched by its influence. For example, the city of Alexandria in Egypt, named after Alexander, acquired a reputation for being the cultural capital of the world and a 'showcase' for the 'Oikumene', the 'new society'. Its museum and library were the equal of any of that time and were the meeting places for many famous scholars and thinkers.

Hand in hand with all this went the widespread use of a version of the Greek language known as the 'Koine', as distinct from the classical Greek, for most business and social affairs, and many Jews found themselves speaking Greek far more often and more easily than their own tongue. So much so, that not long after the death of Alexander scholars began the task of translating parts of the Hebrew scriptures, especially the Torah, into Greek for, it was said, 'the benefit of all'. This was completed in about 250 BC and became known as the Septuagint, because it was said to have been done by seventy scholars. Also, of course, when the Epistles and Gospels of the New Testament appeared, Greek was the language in which they were written.

So it was that Greek fashions of dress, thought, ideals, architecture and entertainment became the acceptable way of life for millions in Alexander's brave new world. Everywhere Greek cities sprang up, either newly-formed or old ones transformed, such as Antioch and Tarsus, and each bearing the 'hallmarks' of Hellenism – theatres, gymnasia, baths, arcades, senates, and so on. Many Jews came to terms with this new culture, especially in the field of business and commercial affairs, even to the extent of giving up their own Jewish customs and fully accepting the Greek life-style.

Not everyone, however, was willing to jump aboard this new band-wagon, without asking who was driving it and where it was supposed to be heading. Far from welcoming this wave of new ideas and outlook, many Jews saw it as far more permissive than progressive and were more fearful than favourable towards its new 'freedoms'. Some said, rather cautiously, that they wanted to know much more about the movement before committing themselves to it, whilst others, more outspoken, resented and resisted it strongly, both for national and religious reasons. In Jerusalem itself, there were very divided opinions as to the delights or dangers of Hellenism, some seeing in it things they thought admirable, others regarding it as a grave threat to their traditional values and beliefs. Some sat on the fence, saying they preferred a more 'middle of the road' approach, but seemed more afraid of being labelled 'intolerant' than 'immoral'.

After Alexander's death, Hellenism continued to spread, amidst mounting confusion, corruption and conflict, as his empire was divided up into four kingdoms. Of these the people in Palestine were only affected by the Ptolemies in Egypt, who ruled for over a century, and the Seleucid, or Syrian rule, which, under Antiochus III took over in 198 BC. Antiochus did not lay any new burdens upon the Jewish people, but Antiochus IV, who became king in 175 BC, certainly did! He was known as 'Epiphanes', which meant 'a god', but he soon began to behave in a most ungodlike manner! No sooner had he assumed power than he was offered support from what the writer of the First Book of Maccabees calls 'wicked men', who had 'disowned the coven-ant and had sold themselves to do evil' (Macc. 1.15). By this he meant that they were so anxious to further the Greek cause that they asked permission from the King to build a gym-nasium in Jerusalem, in order to 'practice the customs of the heathen'. Permission was gladly granted and soon, as the writer bitterly comments, 'even the priests no longer had courage to serve at the altar, but despising the temple they neglect the sacrifices ... liking the glory of the Greeks best'.

Encouraged by all this, a man named Jason went to Antiochus and offered him a huge bribe if the king would appoint him high priest in Jerusalem. Since Jason was a very keen Hellenist, Antiochus accepted the bribe and appointed him, but many Jews, outraged at this kind of selection procedure, rose up in protest and the new king took terrible revenge. Not only did he murder many of the protesters, but decreed that in future all Jewish sacrifices at the temple should cease and be replaced by sacrifices of pigs and other unclean beasts. Circumcision of Jewish boys had got to stop and the Sabbath was to be disregarded. All this was 'to pollute the sanctuary and all their souls, that they may forget the law and change their rules'. Any Jew who didn't obey faced death. The new decree was enforced in every city and anyone found in possession of Jewish scriptures was executed and all the books burnt. On the 25th day of Chisleu (December), heathen offerings, probably pigs, were made on the altar in the temple and the temple itself rededicated to Zeus (I Macc. 1.59).

So the stage was set for revolution and for a fight for the revival of national hope and faith. It just needed a spark to start the blaze and this was provided in the little village of Modin, up in the hills a few miles north-west of Jerusalem. A Greek official arrived one day and demanded that all the inhabitants take part in a pagan sacrifice. A Jewish priest came forward to help with the sacrifice, but the head man of the village, Mattathias, incensed by the sight, ran forward and killed both the priest and the Greek official. He then fled to the hills with his five sons and began a guerilla movement against the Greeks which was to last for a long time, led first by Mattathias, then by his eldest son, Judas, known as 'Maccabeus' the 'Hammerer'. At first the revolt seemed to be successful and there was a feeling of hope and optimism, but then despair began to set in as the struggle began to lose momentum and many Jews began to wonder what sort of vengeance Antiochus would take if he regained control. It was in this kind of situation and against a background of anxiety and apprehension that an unknown writer penned this book of Daniel, using for his hero the name of one who, according to the book of Ezekiel (14.20), was a particularly pious Jew.

The purpose of the writer was plain – to encourage the faithful Jews to hold fast to their loyalty to God and not lose faith in the future. It was a call for courage at a time of great crisis and a demand to stand firm on religious principles, whatever the cost or consequence. We know nothing about the writer except that he was very probably a member of the sect known as the 'Hasidim', or 'pious ones', who demanded loyalty to the Torah above all else and who may well have been the forerunners of the later 'Pharisees'. Whoever he was, he was certainly well aware that fear of the future loomed large in the minds of his readers. They were in great danger not only of their lives, but of having their religious heritage taken away and the faith of their fathers destroyed. To meet that danger they wanted more than pious platitudes or arguments about political parties. They needed a new kind of religious resolve and re-armament. They badly wanted a new moral leadership and a real re-affirmation of their religious ideals. They required a better relationship with God and a revival of spiritual power which would enable them to meet the challenge of paganism.

It was this kind of need that the writer of Daniel is determined to meet. He doesn't preach a vague gospel of so-called 'tolerance' which is often akin to cowardice. He knew very well that unless and until the fundamental facts of the faith were restated firmly and men of greater moral character and courage were found, all hope and talk of a better future was a waste of time. He can be, and sometimes is, criticized on the grounds of his fiery nationalism and seemingly narrow outlook, but at least he had no time for the easy optimism which preaches progress and peace when there is neither, or a pessimism which sees doom and destruction as inevitable. He was not a dealer in dubious devices for telling the future. He looked at the present and faced it squarely. He saw people who were being terribly persecuted for their faith and saw that what was needed was a belief in a God who would never forsake them, whatever happened. His readers needed reminding that Antiochus and his regimes do not have the last word.

So, since it was not unusual, at the time when this book was written, to use as a 'hero' a figure from ancient Jewish tradition, the writer chooses Daniel, the pious person referred to in the book of Ezekiel (Ezek. 14.14; 28.3). He sets the six stories of Daniel and his friends (chs. 1–6) in the court at Babylon, with the first four being put in the reign of Nebuchadnezzar, King of Babylon from 605 BC–562 BC, the fifth one in the time of Belshazzar, supposedly Nebuchadnezzar's successor, and the sixth during the time of a conqueror of Babylon, referred to as Darius the Mede. The important thing, however, is not when the stories are set, but the time when the book was actually written and the circumstances in which it appeared.

There seems general agreement amongst scholars that the book is set in the court of Babylon during the time of the Exile (586–539 BC), not for historical accuracy but to show that faithful Jews, represented in the stories by Daniel and his friends, could remain loyal to their religious principles even under the kind of conditions which prevailed during that Exile. By doing this, the writer had made the kind of historical errors that one might expect if he were looking back over some four hundred years and therefore the records and memories had become somewhat blurred. For example, Nebuchadnezzar did not take Jerusalem in the third year of the reign of Jehoiakim, as stated in the opening verses of ch. 1, nor was it that king who was taken into captivity to Babylon. But the writer's purpose was not to write, or re-write history. It was to give a much needed boost to the sagging morale of his fellow men. He was using the Babylonian setting to show that what had happened to many Jews during the Exile in Babylon had a meaning for those who were anxious about the activities of Antiochus.

Having set the scene in this way, the writer gives a 'prologue', (1.1–5), to show how certain Jews who had been taken to Babylon – 'young men of good looks and physique, well-informed and intelligent' – were set aside to be trained for royal service. The training was to last for three years and would 'instruct them in the literature and language of the Babylonians'. During this time they would be given food and wine from the royal table. Such a prologue would readily be seen symbolically as representing the way in which many young Jews during the time of Antiochus were being tempted away from the Jewish Faith – and Jewish food – by the temptations and attractions of a foreign philosophy and customs.

Among these young men who had been selected for this special training, the writer puts the spotlight on four and weaves his stories around them. Their Jewish names were changed to Babylonian names. Daniel became Belshazzar, though it reverted to Daniel later, but his three friends became Shadrach, Messhach and Abednego. Changing their names, however, did little to change their religious principles. They blankly refused to defile themselves by eating what to them was 'unclean' food, whatever its attractions, and the readers would quickly see the connection between this and the attempts by Antiochus to persuade Jews to abandon their strict food laws, as set out in Lev. 11. Many were already resisting strongly, as the writer of I Macc. made clear. 'Many in Israel were fully resolved not to eat any unclean thing ... they chose rather to die' (I Macc. 1.62), and the example of Daniel would give them great encouragement.

The four young men in the story said they preferred a simpler vegetable diet, with only water to drink, which seemed very plain but on which they prospered. So much so that despite their refusal to eat the palace food, the king 'found them ten times better than his own magicians on any matter calling for intelligence and judgment'. This may possibly have been something to do with their diet, but to the readers it would be seen as much more to do with the discipline of strict obedience to the Torah being much better for their minds than Hellenistic Wisdom. Also, it must be borne in mind that this story was written at a time when Antiochus had made even possession of a copy of the Torah a capital offence.

Then came confrontation, in ch. 2, when the king had a dream, and here the parallels with the Joseph stories in Genesis are pretty strong. None of Nebuchadnezzar's magicians could interpret the dream, which was not really so surprising, since he refused to say what the dream was, but he flew into a rage and ordered the execution of all the wise men. However, Daniel (again like Joseph) was able to interpret the dream, because the answer had been revealed to him in a vision, though the interpretation was, to say the least, somewhat strange. In the dream, the king had seen a massive image, towering above him and 'fearful to behold'. Its head was made of gold, its chest of silver, thighs of bronze and the feet and legs 'part iron and part clay'. Even as the king had gazed awestruck upon this strange sight, a huge rock was taken from the mountain, not by human hands, and hurled at the statue, smashing it into fragments. Then the stone which had been thrown 'grew into a great mountain and filled the whole earth'.

Not surprisingly, such a dream has not lacked all kinds of explanations and interpretations, but the one which Daniel gave was that the image represented four kingdoms, with that of Nebuchadnezzar being the 'head of gold', followed by one of silver, which would be inferior, but then the third one, of bronze, would have dominion until the fourth one caused the collapse of the others, because it had 'feet of clay'. These four kingdoms may well have meant that the Babylonian, the Medes, the Persians and then the Greeks, with Alexander as the legs of iron and his generals as the feet of clay, but the message to the readers would have been clear. They were to take heart. The 'iron and clay' of the Greek rule, never as mighty as the 'golden one' of Babylon, would crumble and collapse. Tyrants may boast of their pomp and power but God's power, like the stone taken from the mountain, would shatter the earthly kingdoms and then God's kingdom would grow and 'endure for ever'.

It was a daunting dream, and the king was quite overcome by the interpretation of it. He fell down in homage before Daniel and said, 'Truly your God is indeed a God of Gods', then proceeded to promote Daniel to be ruler over the whole province of Babylon. Again, there are obvious similarities to the Joseph stories and, to the shrewd observer, some improbabilities too. Just as one may wonder how Joseph could have become ruler of Egypt, so here we may ponder how a foreign king would ever have let a Jewish captive gain such a position, or indeed, whether a Jew would have wanted to accept such a post, but to the writer these implications are secondary to the sequel. He is using them as a framework to his story, not as factual history.

However, the dream having been explained, and due reward given, it would seem that all was now well with Daniel and his friends, but since it is only the second chapter, there is obviously much more to be told. The writer has already pointed to some very important truths, including the fact that earthly kngdoms, however sound they might seem, often have feet of clay and that wise men are often found to be fallible. Now he is going to show that arrogance is often followed by disaster and that pride often precedes a fall. He tells how the king's gratitude and even sense of servitude towards Daniel is soon submerged by the sense of his own importance. With the dream of the statue still in his mind, he decides to make a great image of his own and insists that everyone in the kingdom should bow down to it. Daniel and his friends flatly refuse, so the struggle is on again. The writer is reminding his readers that there is no respite from resistance to evil and that to sit down on the sand after the first victory might well mean that the next wave may catch them unawares.

He therefore describes how Daniel decided to face this next storm head on. He and his friends did not waste time wondering, 'Why does God allow this?' or go about grumbling that it was all unfair. They knew that there was no such thing as one victory over evil paying dividends on which they could live for the rest of their lives. A fresh crisis developed and had to be faced. The image which Nebuchadnezzar set up was, according to the story, about thirty metres high and three metres wide, and made of gold though 'overlaid' may well be a better description. It may have been a statue of a Babylonian god, or even of the king himself, but the main thing was that all and sundry, from princes to peasants, were commanded to bow down to it, to the 'accompaniment of all kinds of music'. The penalty for refusing to do homage when the king called the tune was to be thrown into a fiery furnace. So it was really a choice between bowing or burning and, not surprisingly, many decided to bend the knee.

Daniel and his friends, however, refused to come and conform and their absence was quickly reported to the king, though the messengers mention only the names of the three friends, possibly because the writer is reserving Daniel for a special 'solo' part later on, when he is thrown to the lions. The messengers told the king that the three had 'Taken no notice of your command. They will not serve your god or worship your image.' In another fit of rage, the king reminds them of the consequences. 'And what god can save you from my power?' he asks. Their answer was obvious and was what the readers would expect, bearing in mind the attempts made by Antiochus to make the Jews accept pagan worship. 'The God whom we serve,' the three replied. 'He will save us.' Then they added, as a vital post-script, 'But even if not, be it known that we will not serve your god.' Even if God saw fit to let them suffer, or if the enemy seemed to be superior, there would be no giving way, or going back on their resolve.

Flying into another fury, the king ordered the furnace to be heated up to seven times its normal heat and the three friends to be thrown into it. The flames were so fierce that the men who were carrying Shadrach, Messhach and Abednego to the furnace were themselves burned to death in the process. Then came an amazing sight. Not only were the three men seen to be walking about unharmed in the furnace, but a fourth man – 'who looked like a god' – could be seen in with them. They were taken out, 'without a hair of their heads being singed', and the point was very plain. God had not failed them in their ordeal and hour of need. The king was so impressed that he broke into a kind of doxology about 'the most high God' and gives orders that anyone who 'blasphemed against the God of the three men should be torn to pieces'. Again, the point would not be missed. Antiochus had not only tried to force all the Jews to worship Zeus, but had banned all Jewish worship and had issued decrees to enforce the ban. The 'climb-down' on the part of Nebuchadnezzar would be seen as a sign of the eventual re-instatement of their right to worship under Antiochus.

Then, in chapter four, the king has another dream, even more strange than the first one, 'with fantasies and visions which tempted me'. This time, the king tells the story himself and describes how again his own magicians fail to interpret the dream, though this time he does tell them what it had been! So Daniel was sent for and was 'dismayed and dumbfounded' when he was told of the dream. It was a vision of a great tree which grew and grew until its top 'reached to the heavens' – a little like the great cedar tree in Ezekiel 31 – and its foliage provided shelter for birds and beasts. Then a 'watcher', a 'holy one from heaven' appeared and ordered the tree to be chopped down, leaving only the stump, tethered to which was 'one who eat grass like a beast'.

The meaning of all this was apparently pretty clear to Daniel, but he hesitated to tell the king, until Nebuchadnezzar told him, 'Do not let this matter dismay you.' So Daniel told him that the tree, with all its might and strength, represented the kingdom of Nebuchadnezzar. 'That tree O king, is you,' but it was going to be destroyed by a power far greater than itself and the king himself reduced to weakness and insanity. Indeed, according to Daniel's interpretation, he would be 'banished from the society of men, live with the beasts, feed on grass and be drenched with the dew from heaven'. It was going to be a dramatic come-down for the king, but Daniel didn't shirk the task of telling him so and again the implication would not be lost on the readers. If Nebuchadnezzar could be given such a lesson – 'until you have learnt that the most High is lord over the kingdom of men' – how much more could Antiochus be humbled. It was God who controlled history and earthly kings, however arrogant, were no exception to his judgment.

To prepare the king for the judgment, Daniel advised him to 'repent and be generous to the poor', but since nothing happened during the next twelve months, the king apparently thought the danger was past and he was actually walking on the roof of his palace in Babylon, thinking how splendid everything was, when a voice from heaven told him that the prophecy was going to be fulfilled at once. For seven years he suffered insanity and behaved like a beast, until his sanity was restored and again he broke out into a confession, this time saying that God is supreme and that he will rule for ever. His last words (4.37) were, 'I, Nebuchadnezzar, praise, honour and glorify the King of Heaven. Everything he does is right and he can humble anyone who is proud.' So he leaves the stage of these stories, acknowledging that he is nothing in the sight of God.

In the next scene, chapter five, Nebuchadnezzar's son, Belshazzar, called 'king' by the writer, but actually never more than a caretaker for the kingdom whilst his father was away in Arabia, was giving a grand feast to which he had invited a thousand noblemen. When the party was in full swing, the king commanded that the golden drinking vessels taken from the temple in Jerusalem when the city had been sacked and looted in 586 BC, should be brought into the hall so that the king, noblemen and concubines could all drink from them. As they indulged in drunken debauchery, they 'praised gods made of gold, silver, wood and stone'. Such desecration, according to the writer, demanded dramatic divine intervention and it came in the shape of a ghostly hand which suddenly appeared and slowly wrote some strange words on the walls of the banqueting hall. When he saw this, Belshazzar 'turned pale and went limp and his knees knocked together', even before he knew what the message meant!

Again, the same pattern is followed, as the king sends for the magicians to decipher the words, but they could not and this time it was the queen who suggested sending for Daniel, because, she said, 'He has the spirit of the holy God in him.' When Daniel arrived he was offered all kinds of rewards if he could read the writing, but he curtly told the king to keep his gold and his gifts. The words on the wall were *MENE, MENE, TEKEL, PARSIN*, though some versions omit one MENE. The translation didn't seem to cause Daniel much difficulty, but scholars seem to have been wondering what exactly the message meant ever since. It all depends on how the Aramaic words are 'pointed', or punctuated. They could mean 'weights', with the MN the mina, TGL the shekel and PRS the half-mina. Or they could mean 'to number', 'to weigh', 'to divide'. Such double meanings were not uncommon and in the writing of both Jeremiah and Amos, for example, we see the same device used. Daniel apparently used both ideas, for he told the king that the words meant that God has 'Numbered the days of your kingdom, you have been weighed in the balance and found wanting, and your kingdom will be divided up between the Medes and the Persians'.

One can hardly imagine that the king was too delighted at such a decoding of the writing on the wall, but nevertheless he heaped gifts upon Daniel and made him 'third power in the kingdom'. Possibly he thought that such a display of goodwill might delay the fulfilment of the prophecy, but it didn't and that very night he died, though the writer does not say how, and 'Darius the Mede' seized power. Actually the idea of a Median kingdom coming between the Babylonian and Persian rule is another error on the writer's part and he seems to be confused between Cyrus, who captured Babylon in 538 BC and Darius I who took over in 520 BC. But again, the writer is not reconstructing history; if he had he would have been more careful. He is far more interested in 'setting up' the final scene, in chapter six, in which Daniel is thrown into the lions' den, thereby facing the same kind of ordeal as his three friends had faced in the furnace. They had defied a king's decree and now Daniel was about to do the same.

It seems that Darius decided, when he became king, to appoint 120 governors throughout the kingdom and to make Daniel an overseer over these governors, presumably as a reward for deciphering the writing on the wall. Daniel, however, proved so satisfactory that Darius considered putting him in charge of all the kingdom. Such a possibility soon aroused the jealousy of the other governors and they spared no effort to try and find fault with Daniel, but they failed 'because he was so reliable and faithful to his trust'. So they came to the conclusion that there would be no charge to bring against 'this Daniel' unless they could 'find one in his religion'. They therefore persuaded Darius to issue a decree 'forbidding anyone to make any request of a god'. Obviously the governors knew of Daniel's daily practice of private prayer and thought they had devised a way to bring about his downfall. The king issued the order and once it was given it was unalterable, 'for the law of the Medes and Persians stands forever'.

The writer is raising the issue which every religious conscience has to face sooner or later: whether to maintain important principles in the face of persecution, or to trim one's sails, for the sake of compromise or tolerance, to suit the prevailing wind. Daniel was brought before Darius and the king did his best to try and make the young man change his attitude, since he was 'greatly distressed' to learn that Daniel was defying the decree and was 'kneeling down three times a day before windows which opened towards Jerusalem and offering prayers to God'. The point of this would not be lost on the readers, since just as the Jews had been cut off from temple worship in Jerusalem during the Exile in Babylon, Antiochus was trying to do the same. According to I Macc. 1.42 he had sent letters to the whole people that 'everyone should leave his own laws'. He had forbidden public temple worship, but many Jews worshipped secretly, regardless of the consequences if they were caught. The writer of the book of Daniel is reminding them that if they are denied public worship they must continue in private devotions.

It could, of course, be said that Daniel could have avoided the confrontation by making his daily prayers even more secret and instead of 'opening the windows' he could have kept them closed and prayed in seclusion. Surely, it might be argued, it wouldn't have made much difference. But to what extent is such compromise ever justified? Would not such an action have meant a trading in of integrity for the sake of safety? Are there not times when faith demands a dedication that does not fear the consequences? A look at the lives of such people as Dietrich Bonhoeffer and Martin Niemoller, for example, will surely show that there is. In the USSR, in 1929, Stalin's Law on Religious Association, in which every form of religious observance and education was offically banned, in public or in private, was followed by a terrible persecution in which many thousands of Christians were imprisoned and put to death, but through it all many continued to witness and worship, just as they do today in countries like Albania, Bulgaria and Czechoslovakia, despite severe restrictions and considerable opposition, and certainly the book of Daniel can be seen as relevant in these peoples' situation and experience.

Darius tried all day to persuade Daniel to change his mind, but at sunset the governors reminded the king of the decree and that time had now run out. So Daniel was thrown into a pit, probably a kind of cistern in the ground, with a heavy stone on the top which was sealed with the king's seal, to make sure it was not interfered with, and then he was left to the lions. Apparently Darius had a very restless night and early next morning he went to the pit, 'in fear and trembling', to see what had happened to Daniel. He called out, 'Was the God you serve able to save you from the lions?' To which Daniel repied, 'God sent an angel to shut the mouths of the lions, so that they would not hurt me.' The king, it says, was overjoyed and immediately gave orders for Daniel to be taken from the pit. When the servants did this, they saw that he was not harmed in any way, 'because he had trusted in God'. Some sceptics may say that it was more likely because the lions had been previously fed and were therefore not hungry, but the writer precludes this by telling how when Daniel's accusers were thrown into the den – which was the typical 'martyr motif', where the would-be tormenters suffer the same fate as their intended victim – they were devoured before they could even reach the floor of the pit!

So the first half of the book ends (6. 25–28), with the king issuing another decree, this time that 'everyone should reverence the God of Daniel, for he is the living God'. That was the word which his readers would want to hear. Their God was a God who could and would save them from their enemies, whether it be Nebuchadnezzar, Darius or Antiochus. The writer had set his story in the past, but the message and moral were for the present. He focuses on the people's persecutions and tells them not to lose hope and faith. He then looks to the future and sees God's purpose and plan unfolding on the stage of history. The canvas was large, but God was the artist. Earthly kingdoms may rise and fall but God's plans were pre-arranged and 'what is determined shall be done'.

In this sense, the book is apocalyptic, for it looks to a future where justice and peace shall prevail because God is in control. We may not fully agree with the writer's concept of history and we may think his heroes are more ideal than real, but one thing is clear. He puts tyranny and persecution in perspective. He believes that however the forces of evil and hatred seem to be carrying all before them, they will not succeed. He also reminds his readers that a faith that does not make demands will not make much progress. Such truths were not just timely, they are timeless, and the story of Daniel is seen as being concerned with a lot more than just a lions' den!